ANWAR TRIUMPHS

ANWAR TRIUMPHS

THE ASCENT OF MALAYSIA'S TENTH PRIME MINISTER AGAINST ALL ODDS

MARK TROWELL KC

Marshall Cavendish
Editions

Published by Marshall Cavendish Editions
An imprint of Marshall Cavendish International

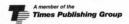

A member of the
Times Publishing Group

Other Marshall Cavendish Offices
Marshall Cavendish Corporation, 800 Westchester Ave, Suite N-641, Rye Brook, NY 10573, USA • Marshall Cavendish International (Thailand) Co Ltd, 253 Asoke, 16th Floor, Sukhumvit 21 Road, Klongtoey Nua, Wattana, Bangkok 10110, Thailand • Marshall Cavendish (Malaysia) Sdn Bhd, Times Subang, Lot 46, Subang Hi-Tech Industrial Park, Batu Tiga, 40000 Shah Alam, Selangor Darul Ehsan, Malaysia

Marshall Cavendish is a registered trademark of Times Publishing Limited

National Library Board Singapore Cataloguing in Publication Data
Name(s): Trowell, Mark, author.
Title: Anwar triumphs : the ascent of Malaysia's tenth prime minister against all odds / Mark Trowell.
Description: Singapore : Marshall Cavendish Editions, [2023]
Identifier(s): ISBN 978-981-5113-07-5 (paperback)
Subject(s): LCSH: Anwar Ibrahim, 1947- | Malaysia--Politics and government--21st century. | Prime ministers--Malaysia.
Classification: DDC 320.9595--dc23

Printed in Malaysia by Times Offset Malaysia

Cover photo by Vincent Thian/Pool via REUTERS
All cartoons by Zunar
All photographs courtesy of Mark Trowell and Anwar Ibrahim, except page 136 (YuriAbas/Shutterstock) and page 140 (Abdul Razak Latif/Shutterstock).

To the memory of my late mother,
Patricia Aileen Powell.

This book is also dedicated to my friends
Datuk David Yeoh Eng Hock,
the late David Kingsley Malcolm AC QC
and the late Datuk Michael Bong Thiam Joon

Contents

Foreword

The year 2008 was a turbulent time for Malaysia, as every year seemed to be, with the same old cronyism and corruption. The domestic economy experienced the full impact of the global recession.

During another financial crisis ten years earlier, Prime Minister Mahathir had sacked his deputy Anwar Ibrahim from office for "sexual misconduct". Anwar was not immediately charged, but toured the country agitating for reform, urging that Mahathir resign.

After leading a huge rally at Merdeka Square on 20 September 1998, Anwar was finally arrested with hundreds of other demonstrators and charged under the Internal Security Act with illegal assembly and related offences. That was the birth of the *Reformasi* movement.

Nine days later, Anwar was brought to court and charged with sodomy and corruption. He appeared with noticeable injuries, having been beaten by the then Inspector-General of Police. The images of Anwar outside the court with a neck brace and black eye, and with his arm raised in a salute of defiance, appeared in newspapers around the world. It is an image of defiance against corruption that is still vivid in people's memory.

Anwar was convicted after trial and sentenced to prison in April 1999. Mahathir retained power at the national election in November that year and would finally retire from office in October 2003. Anwar was later released after a successful appeal against conviction in 2004. More difficulties were to come over the next 18 years that would test his mettle and resilience.

Returning to the year 2008, I recall it because I gave a speech at Ipoh, Perak, as part of the campaign supporting Anwar for the general election that year.

I had been a senator for six years with the Malaysian Chinese Association, which was part of the ruling coalition Barisan Nasional, but left politics in 1983 because I could no longer support the values of my old party. Things just did not seem to change.

Mahathir's vision for Malaysia was bound up in racial divisions and privileges for the *Bumiputera*. He had changed Malaysia's economic fortunes for the better, which was a significant achievement, but it was really a system benefiting the wealthy and privileged. I suppose I was one of them, but I wanted more for my country.

I had no intention of returning to politics until I met Anwar Ibrahim in London in 2007. I had fixed negative opinions of him from my years in parliament, however, after a lengthy conversation with him, I became a supporter.

He was no longer the young Muslim firebrand agitator or UMNO politician, but someone who had experienced hardship and grown wiser and more tolerant. I saw Anwar as someone who could change the future of Malaysia.

This is what I told the assembled crowd at Ipoh on that campaign rally in 2008. It still resonates today:

The reason I went back into politics is because I met Anwar, through Senator Michael Bong, in my son's restaurant in London and we had a heart-to-heart talk. To be honest with you, when I was a senator in Barisan Nasional, we were all indoctrinated with: "Oh, you cannot trust Anwar. He is a terrible man. His ambition is to be prime minister. He doesn't worry about the country. He will sell the country to the Americans."

I had a very frank talk with Anwar. We sat down and chatted for three to four hours and he said to me, "David, whatever I said when I was in UMNO, I don't deny, but I've been in jail for six long years, and during that time I've learnt so much, and I think a man needs a second chance." Don't you think everyone needs a second chance?

I remember when I was a young man in the 1950s to 1960s – we ate and slept with our Malay friends. We had no problem with that. Why are we having these racial problems in our universities and everywhere? Why? Because UMNO has divided the races. It has learnt from the British how to divide and rule.

That was true, and I was referring to a time when the prime minister was Tunku Abdul Rahman, when there was no racial-based politics to divide the community. It had started to change after the civil disturbances in May 1969. Mahathir was masterful at playing "race politics" and exploiting racial division, and it kept him in power for more than 20 years.

The remnants of Mahathir's rule by racial division are still in place. Unlike other multiracial countries, Malaysians when completing documents are asked to indicate their race, rather than simply stating they are Malaysians. That is wrong, and it should change.

Anwar is different. He accepts racial diversity and yet preaches inter-ethnic harmony. When he talks about disadvantage, it's not just about the poor Malays, but all of whom are disadvantaged, whether they are Malay, Chinese or Indian. When he talks about prosperity, it's about prosperity for all Malaysians.

In my speech in 2008 to the crowd before GE12 at Ipoh, I reminded them that Barisan Nasional had been in power for 52 years. I asked them to give Pakatan Rakyat just ten per cent of that time, or five years, and if we failed, then they could just get rid of us.

We almost got that chance later that year in the national election GE12, when the incumbent Barisan Nasional regime for the first time since 1969 did not receive its customary two-thirds majority in the lower house in parliament, which would allow it to change the Constitution at will.

Opposition DAP leader Lim Kit Siang called it a "tsunami", but it was not enough to sweep the government from office. That did not happen until a decade later, when the opposition coalition, known as Pakatan Harapan, ousted the Barisan Nasional coalition led by Prime Minister Najib Razak, which had ruled Malaysia since 1957.

A lot has happened in those ten years, including Anwar again being falsely charged and convicted in an attempt to keep him out of politics in 2008. He was sent to prison once more but emerged after a royal pardon in 2018. In the few years following, there was much turmoil and scandal, but finally, Anwar is now prime minister of Malaysia.

I still feel the same about him, all these years later. I have never had any cause to doubt his commitment to all Malaysians. I never doubted that he would ultimately lead Malaysia. I do not doubt he will be a great prime minister, finally triumphing after much adversity.

A Bollywood script could not have been more dramatic with the twists and turns of events. In a personal sense, his triumph has come at a terrible cost for himself and his family because of his long periods of imprisonment, and yet surely his emergence as prime minister is a tribute to his resilience, courage and determination to lead his country. It is a true "Mandela" moment – from a prison cell to being the leader of his country.

Datuk David Yeoh Eng Hock

REFORMASI

Cartoon by Zunar

Introduction

This book completes the cycle of my accounts of the roller-coaster life of Anwar Ibrahim that began with my first book *Sodomy II: The Trials of Anwar Ibrahim*, which recorded the second sodomy trial that resulted in his acquittal on 9 January 2012.

My second book, *The Prosecution of Anwar Ibrahim: The Final Play*, covered the events surrounding the Federal Court's shock decision to uphold the Prosecution's appeal of the acquittal, which resulted in Anwar's conviction and imprisonment on 10 February 2015.

The final book in the trilogy was entitled *Anwar Returns: The Final Twist*. It covered the 1MDB scandal and collapse of the UMNO regime, and the election of the Mahathir-Anwar coalition on 9 May 2018 at GE14. It also covered the King's pardon of Anwar and his immediate release from prison on 16 May 2018, after having served almost three years of his sentence.

The four years following Anwar's release have been dramatic and chaotic. This book records the key events over that time, including the collapse of the Pakatan Harapan coalition of Mahathir-Anwar and the effective return to power of UMNO, in coalition with defectors from Pakatan Harapan and others.

It also covers the turmoil after Mahathir's shock resignation as prime minister in February 2020, that upended the country's politics; the contest with his old rival Anwar; the political betrayal by former allies and the deals to secure power; the change of prime ministers; and the sensational conviction and jailing of former prime minister Najib Razak for corruption.

All of these happenings led to the hung parliament result of GE15 and the ultimate appointment by the King of Anwar Ibrahim as the tenth prime minister of Malaysia. It has been a personal triumph for him. It has been against all odds, if you consider the extraordinary events since Mahathir sacked him from office in 1998.

Mark Trowell KC

CHAPTER 1

Conversation with
Prime Minister Anwar Ibrahim
(27 January 2023)

The conversation with the prime minister took place in the Prime Minister's Office, Putrajaya.

Mark: Good afternoon, Prime Minister. Thank you for making yourself available for this interview during what must be a busy time for you.

Anwar: Delighted to do so.

Mark: May I first ask what is it like achieving the office of prime minister after such a long time?

Anwar: Well, because you wait, you wait for such a long time. It is ... what should I say? Not so much excitement in a sense, as thank God, I'm back to work.

Mark: Yes.

Anwar: Sometimes it's just sitting down and then thinking, my God, I'm in this office.

Mark: I imagine it's been hectic these last few months?

Anwar: Oh yes, it's been hectic, but things are settling down. I thought it would settle down in one month. Now it's been two months.

SETTING AN EXAMPLE

Mark: Before we begin the interview, I want to pass on the numerous greetings from many of the people I have spoken to since being here, particularly the staff at my hotel. They know I've written books about your struggle and they say: "You're going to see the boss? Yes, tell him we support him."

Anwar: Okay.

Mark: So, they send their best wishes to you.

Anwar: Oh, thank you. And, in that sense, it's good, good because I get positive vibes from the people, particularly about the many changes, but it's early days.

Mark: Well, this one young hotel staff member told me it was his first vote. You really impressed him when you refused to accept the expensive Mercedes S600 limousine that had been ordered as the official car by the Prime Minister's Department before you came into office.

Anwar: Mmm.

Mark: He said: "No one does that in Malaysia."

Anwar: Mmm, but now I regret it. (both laugh) Because they gave me an old Proton and I have this bad back, you know, and there is a problem with the suspension ... I take whatever car is available. There's a Toyota Camry there. Okay, I've got to survive on that, you see! (laughs)

Mark: You have had significant back and shoulder pain for at least 20 years made worse by imprisonment and being beaten by the police when in custody in 1999. You've also had surgery a number of times, is that right?

Anwar: That's right.

Mark: But you had a Jaguar when you were leader of the opposition?

Anwar: Yes. A Jaguar. And then, in fact, there was a [BMW] Seven Series with a friend of mine from Bangsar, who gave it to me just before the elections to use during the elections. So as prime minister, I'm back to a Proton with poor suspension. It's an old car, it's a 12-year-old Proton. I said: "Oh my God." And then we changed to the Camry.

Mark: Man of the people?

Anwar: Yes, I know. I needed to set an example, particularly when a lot of people are struggling financially. It's a small thing, but my way of setting an example.

Anwar had been deputy prime minister under Mahathir from 1993 to 1998. He was expected to succeed Mahathir as prime minister, but their once close relationship deteriorated as Anwar sought to introduce radical reforms as acting PM (while Mahathir was on a two-month holiday). There was conflict over their differing views on governance, and Anwar's criticism of the widespread culture of nepotism and cronyism angered Mahathir.

The 1997 Asian Financial Crisis brought the conflict between them to a head. As finance minister, Anwar supported the International Monetary Fund plan introducing an austerity programme that cut government spending by 18 per cent, cut ministerial salaries and deferred major projects, despite "mega projects" being the cornerstone of Mahathir's development strategy.

Anwar's fall from power came quickly, when on 2 September 1998, he was sacked from the Cabinet. Less than two weeks later, he was arrested under the draconian Internal Security Act (ISA) and later charged with corruption and sodomy. While in custody, he was beaten by the Inspector-General of Police, emerging to face charges in court with facial bruising and in a neck brace.

WHAT MIGHT HAVE BEEN?

Mark: Let me ask you this, do you think you're better placed to be prime minister now than you would've been, say in 1999? I mean, you're a different person.

Anwar: In a sense, better now. Yes, in a way. I would have done things differently then, than now. And now (gently taps table thrice), in fact, I'm in better shape. I'm just tougher. I just don't care. You know what I mean? Like say, for corruption those days, had I taken over, say in 1999, Najib would have been my deputy. So, in hindsight, okay, a lot of trials, the periods of imprisonment, a lot of misery for my family, but I think it ends well, in a sense. I mean, there's still time. It's too early, but we've got the full support of the Malay rulers and a lot of voters.

EXTENT OF CORRUPTION

Mark: Is the burden of responsibility as prime minister much different from being opposition leader?

Anwar: Yes. There are the intelligence briefings, national security, and the economic issues to deal with. We're in a mess now. It's terrible. In every field, the amount of corruption is just shocking (gently slaps hand on table). We've been very strong on that in the past, right?

Mark: Yes, you have.

Anwar: So, when I look at the files, it's worse. Much worse!

Mark: Worse than you imagined?

Anwar: Yes. Worse. Much worse.

Anwar had in the few months after his appointment as prime minister returned to the theme of eradicating corruption, which he claimed had adversely impacted the economy and held back the financial development and reputation of Malaysia.

On the morning of our interview, Anwar had given a speech at the Associated Chinese Chambers of Commerce and Industry (ACCCIM) at Jalan Ampang, Kuala Lumpur, at which he said:[1]

---

1   *Malay Mail*, 28 January 2023

People can harp upon issues of race or religion, to me, it's completely irrelevant. It's a way and attempt by political leaders to disguise and hijack the central issues of governance in this country. They are going to appeal to the race, including the Malays, that their position, their power base is challenged.

Now my answer to that question is, it is not being challenged by Malay businessmen or Chinese businessmen or Indian businessmen or Sabah, Sarawak. The Malay survival is being threatened by a corrupt system, a greedy coterie of leaders who have been stealing public funds from this country, so we will have to continue to work together to make sure we save this country from corruption.

He went on to say:

You in the business community know precisely what I'm talking about, every deal, every contract, they will attempt, and of course in the process, huge commissions and bribery.

It's not for me to conduct investigations or prosecute, but I trust the authorities will not delay this, because we are not talking about [the] political survival of an individual or party or a government, we are talking about the survival of this great nation of Malaysia for all Malaysians in this country.

MUHYIDDIN'S TACTICAL MISTAKE

When faced with a hung parliament after GE15, which failed to produce a party that could command a simple majority, the King called for a unity government, comprising a cross-coalition between Muhyiddin's Perikatan Nasional (PN) and Anwar's Pakatan Harapan (PH). He made the request after a one-hour audience with the two leaders.

Both parties had emerged from the polls with the largest blocs of seats in parliament, but neither had sufficient votes to have the 222 seats required for a majority. Anwar said he "accepted the spirit of a unity government", but Muhyiddin immediately rejected the proposal, maintaining he had sufficient support to become prime minister.[2]

> **Mark:** Muhyiddin made a tactical mistake, didn't he, by saying he wouldn't join a unity government, so it was much easier for the King to appoint you, as you had more parliamentary seats?
>
> **Anwar:** Yes, they had 71, we had 82.
>
> **Mark:** Yes. They got less numbers, but I think the critical thing was, you were prepared to lead a unity government.
>
> **Anwar:** Yes. He refused to be associated with Pakatan Harapan.
>
> **Mark:** Yes, so he paid the price.
>
> **Anwar:** He paid the price.

UMNO'S INTERNAL ISSUES

> **Mark:** It's interesting to see what's happening internally with UMNO. They are going to expel Khairy Jamaluddin and suspend others for disloyalty to the party?
>
> **Anwar:** Mmm.
>
> **Mark:** How the mighty have fallen.

There had been internal hostilities within UMNO's senior ranks as some had challenged and criticised the party leadership, one of whom was Ahmad Zahid Hamidi, the party president and deputy prime minister in the Pakatan Harapan alliance government. It had resulted in sackings and suspension of party membership for disciplinary breaches on 27 January 2023. Those expelled or suspended included former ministers Khairy Jamaluddin, Moh Omar and Hishammuddin. At the time of the interview, it was expected to happen, but did not until later that day. Observers said that the upcoming party elections prompted the purge.

I tried to draw Anwar into commenting on what was foreshadowed to happen that day in UMNO, but he was clearly reluctant to speak about the internal affairs of another party, which was also part of the Pakatan Harapan alliance.

The most controversial appointment was that of BN's Ahmad Zahid Hamidi as one of the deputy prime ministers. Anwar was to explain his reasons for doing so in a television interview on Bloomberg TV on 10 February 2023, the excerpts of which are reproduced in Chapter 10 of this book.

> **Anwar:** Yes. But you know, it is also the politics of incumbency. For example, I was opposition leader and more popular in some areas, but you know, with a position, it's different. I can sense, for example, I go to the mosque on Friday, right? After prayers, there will be people swarming around me. In the past, there would be like half of the mosque who would come, and then the rest would just disappear quietly.

> **Mark:** You mean everybody wants to be your friend now that you're prime minister?

Anwar: Of course. (softly) Or at least they are quite decent and polite, and I find hundreds of people just apologising, in the Malay word, *maaf*, "I'm sorry, I'm sorry, I'm sorry. I didn't ask ..."

Mark: For what? Your treatment in the past?

Anwar: Well, they might have said something nasty or they ...

Mark: Ahh ...

Anwar: Yes. Yes, many. But, of course, I don't pursue it, *sudah lah*, I say never mind, move on! (waves a hand)

DR WAN AZIZAH WAN ISMAIL

Mark: I want to ask you about Wan Azizah. One of the reasons she's on the draft cover of the new book is because when you think about it, you really couldn't have done it without her, could you?

Anwar: No.

Mark: I mean, she was party president.

Anwar: Yes.

Mark: She was a member of parliament.

Anwar: She was ... yes.

Mark: Deputy prime minister.

Anwar: Yes, fiercely so ...

Mark: Mother.

Anwar: Mother. Yes. Took care of the children.

Mark: Wife and ...

Anwar: Strong. And at no point did she ever give up. (taps on table)

Mark: I'm going to make special mention of her ...

Anwar: It'd be great. Yes. She deserves that. She does.

Mark: Yes, because I asked you when I interviewed you in 2018, whether as deputy prime minister she was now officially "the boss". Certainly, in politics, she was your boss, and even at home? You had diplomatically replied that there were no gender issues at home, right? You wouldn't admit she was the boss in the house? (both laugh) But seriously, her support and devotion was critical whether you were in prison or not?

Anwar: Mmm. It was very helpful. Now I realise.

Exclusive: Chapter 8 of this book features an interview with Dr Wan Azizah Wan Ismail covering a range of personal and political issues.

THE MANDELA EXPERIENCE

Anwar and his family were invited to meet Nelson Mandela in 2004 in Johannesburg, South Africa. He described the meeting as a "profound moment trading stories about our time in prison."[3]

> **Mark:** After the Rivonia trial, Mandela was imprisoned for 18 years. I think your experience may have been worse in some ways because you were in and out of prison. Then there were the constant court battles over 20 years.

> **Anwar:** Yes. It was a bad experience. His experience was different. That's why when I met Mandela, I can still recall that he was emotional and in tears. In tears. When he saw my children and my wife. He was very disturbed.

> **Mark:** Yes.

> **Anwar:** I could sense that. I didn't pursue it, but he said: "Anwar, you're so lucky."

> **Mark:** He meant to have the family support?

> **Anwar:** Yes, because he had the political support from his family, but missed them. There were the prison visits, but he had not seen them growing up.

> **Mark:** You had two periods of imprisonment. You spent a total of what, ten years or more than ten years?

> **Anwar:** Ten ... more than ten and a half years. Crazy, yes. Just to reflect on that, I plan to visit Sungai Buloh Prison.

---

3   Anwar, Facebook, 18 July 2020

Mark: Yes.

Anwar: But I've been just too busy. Maybe in the next week or so.

THE RELATIONSHIP WITH TUN DR MAHATHIR MOHAMAD

Mark: Mahathir is now yesterday's man. I mean, he lost his parliamentary seat in the election.

Anwar: Yes. He actually lost his deposit, not just lost his seat, can you imagine?

Mark: Lost his deposit because his votes were so low, right?

Anwar: Yes!

Mahathir lost his seat of Langkawi in GE15. He managed to garner only 4,566 votes, or 6.8 per cent of total votes cast. He required 12.5 per cent vote threshold to keep his deposit as a candidate, which he lost. In comparison, Mahathir had won 54.9 per cent of the 34,527 votes cast in 2018's GE14. It was a humiliating result for him. It was his first electoral defeat since 1969.

Mark: What happened? Did Malaysia wake up to him?

Anwar: Yes. One must understand the historic significance, in the sense that Langkawi was essentially built by him. It's not just a constituency. The whole area was his baby. The new airport, the developments, tourism, employment and training. Every ambitious opportunity for the locals, he did it for 30 years. After spending billions to build up the island, and people just ditched him. (smacks table gently)

Mark: Does it show how fickle voters are or did they show good judgement?

Anwar: No. People thought, okay, you have done your part, but we have to move on, and probably since he was no longer consistent, his ideas were obsolete and he was becoming more irrelevant. I think essentially that.

Mark: And the young ones wouldn't know him, would they, really?

Anwar: No, they knew him because the prime minister is in textbooks. It was all Mahathir there, that was *our* problem! Because, other than those who actually followed my case, the rest would say, well, Mahathir is a great leader. In the Middle East, most of Asia, African countries, he's the man who could stand up to the Americans! (smacks table gently)

Mark: Well, I mean, I re-read portions of my last book to refresh my memory. When we spoke last time in 2018, you said that you trusted Mahathir because you thought he was committed to reform. Now we know that wasn't true.

Anwar: Yes.

Mark: But, of course, you had no choice, did you?

Anwar: I had no choice.

Mark: I mean, you were in prison. You hadn't been pardoned.

Anwar: Yes.

Mark: Although from what I understand, the King and Wan Azizah were not keen on Mahathir as prime minister? Is that true?

Anwar: Yes. You see, there are two issues there. Firstly, why did I support Mahathir? I wrote a letter to my party colleagues from prison about the serpent and the leopard. This was about the proposal to support Mahathir for the leadership.

Mark: What did you say?

Anwar: So, I said: "Now, you guys have agreed to support Mahathir for the leadership, let me caution you about certain things", which I set out in the letter. This letter is very historically important. I think the letter was in English, except one part in Malay, but they have translated it, and that's when I made reference to: "You are naive to imagine that Mahathir is a reformer." (taps table gently) Oh yes, I said: "We need to forgive him. Move on," I even used the Quranic verse "to forgive him", we must be able to forgive, but we must not be naive.

Exclusive: See extracts from Anwar's letter to his colleagues about the alliance with Mahathir, translated from Malay and reproduced in Chapter 6 of this book.

Mark: Well, Mahathir is still criticising you. He just can't help himself, can he? But he did that to everyone. He did that to former prime ministers Badawi and Najib. It was really whomever was going to be the leader or the prime minister would never be good enough for him. Lim Kit Siang (former DAP leader) has been reported as saying everyone should ignore Mahathir's criticisms and just focus on carrying out as many institutional reforms as possible.

Anwar: I just ignore Mahathir.

But Mahathir was not ignoring Anwar. Despite losing his parliamentary seat in the 2022 general election, the 97-year-old Mahathir continued to snipe at Anwar in the media, accusing him of acting like a dictator; rejecting the Constitution by scuttling a Malay "solidarity rally" at which he was scheduled to speak after several venues cancelled their booking in March 2023; and threatened Anwar with defamation proceedings for suggesting that he had enriched himself and his family when in power.[4]

In an interview with CNBC Indonesia TV, which was aired on 13 January 2023, Anwar said he did not want to entertain any comments made by Dr Mahathir. "The people have chosen and given their mandate to me to do the job. I am focusing on that ... but I also don't want this to be perceived as a never-ending enmity (with Dr Mahathir)," he said in response to a question on his relationship with Mahathir.

During the same interview, which was recorded during his visit to Indonesia, Anwar was also asked about politics in Malaysia, which the prime minister replied was "different from Indonesia and some other countries":[5]

National news agency Bernama reported Mr Anwar as saying "political hostility" in Malaysia has been described as "very sharp", which he said could be due to the legacy of Dr Mahathir's leadership style.

4   *The Straits Times*, 28 March 2023; *South China Morning Post*, 28 March 2023
5   *The Straits Times*, 14 January 2023

"Whoever does not support him (Dr Mahathir) is considered an enemy ... and this situation (sharp political hostility) has continued until now.

"But at least we (the government) acted quickly (by changing to the new political style) by thinking about the country, the future and political stability, and so we succeeded in forming a coalition with a stance of good governance and rejecting corruption and this principle has been agreed upon."

Former prime minister Najib Razak jumped into the argument responding to Mahathir's criticism of Anwar by labelling him a dictator. In a Facebook post on 19 March 2023, he said Mahathir should not be calling others a dictator when he was oppressive during his two tenures as prime minister.

"Who was the one who enforced the Internal Security Act (ISA) and changed the country's Attorney-General, Malaysian Anti-Corruption Commission (MACC) chief and Chief Justice for his own benefit?" Najib asked.[6]

Mark: Let's talk about the leadership transition. Mahathir just stalled for time, didn't he? There was no prospect that he was ever going to hand over the premiership to you.

Anwar: Yes, I had to be realistic at that time. Although, my letters are important because in them I said: "Look, this guy cannot be trusted. Now that you have agreed, I concur. I mean, I've no choice but to agree with you guys," because Kit Siang was also quite instrumental. He wanted to get Mahathir on board. His reason was because he thought Azizah may not be able to have that push.

---

6   *The Straits Times*, 20 March 2023

Mark: Your daughter Nurul Izzah flew to London, didn't she, to complete the deal with Mahathir?

Anwar: Yes. She was furious because she said that probably was a mistake. I said: "No, we have to move on, and then ..."

Mark: But despite Mahathir's treacherous track record, you had to do it.

Anwar: Yes.

Mark: Mahathir signed an agreement about the leadership arrangement?

Anwar: Oh yes, despite my strong criticism against the decision, I was forced to endorse it. Then in negotiations they got him to sign an agreement.

> **Exclusive:** See extracts from the Pakatan Harapan agreement signed by all parties in the alliance, including Mahathir, translated from Malay and reproduced in Chapter 4 of this book.

THE SHERATON MOVE

Mark: In February 2020, the Pakatan Harapan government collapsed after 22 months in power, soon after what was called the "Sheraton Move". That was a meeting at the Sheraton Hotel at Petaling Jaya of those who were opposed to you, led by Azmin Ali? Did Mahathir entice them to cross over?

Anwar: Mmm, yes.

Mark: It was all him?

Anwar: Yes, it was him.

Mark: He was at the meeting of the supreme council of PPBM on 23 February 2020, wasn't he?

Anwar: He was there. Now, the other issue with Mahathir is what he did from the word go, from the beginning, that's why I had to make sure that I was seen to be supportive, and not break up the coalition. So, I went along, but from the beginning, the Cabinet, for example, he didn't consult us.

Mark: Yes, I heard he just made executive decisions.

Anwar: Yes, that's why, you see you have Azmin Ali in the camp.

Mark: At the time, I spoke with some DAP MPs, one of whom was a minister, and asked why they were not supporting you and were prepared to back Mahathir as prime minister? He told me that the government could only survive with Mahathir, and that it was better being in government than opposition.

Anwar: Oh, Karpal would never, never have supported Mahathir. It is good in some ways because, with that experience, the DAP has learnt a lesson, that it's not just you and your party. The Malay reaction was very severe against them.

Mark: Yes.

Anwar: The Malay anger is against the DAP for what happened in the 22 months of government, and how it played out when Mahathir resigned as prime minister. It's not necessarily fair because I think they became so blinded by these attacks.

Mark: But they were all prepared to desert you at one stage and then support Mahathir to stay in government.

Anwar: Yes, and because I refused to have that, we lost government.

Mark: But it was going to end badly anyway?

Anwar: But I said to them, if you do that, then we are finished, for at least one generation.

Mark: Yes.

Anwar: If we had given back the power to Mahathir at that time we were finished, so I was just adamant. I said: "No way will I ever agree." For example, the ethnic Indians rejected us because Mahathir just arrested these guys. Can you imagine, they were arrested under SOSMA [Security Offences (Special Measures) Act], which allows for detention without trial. I argued with the then Attorney-General, Tommy Thomas. I said: "Why?" He said: "No, there's a reason I sign it." I said: "How? You're AG?" You see, that's the problem. All these so-called liberal guys, all change when they turn to power like Latheefa Koya (former MACC Chief). Yes, because they became Mahathir's lackeys.

Mark: I saw Lim Kit Siang's recent comments to the media, when he said: "Don't worry about Mahathir. There's too much reform that needs to be done."

Anwar: Well now, yes, of course. People say: "Yes, just ignore him." In fact, they had even advised me just to ignore him. Do not respond to him.

Mark: Are you happy to talk about Mahathir?

Anwar: It's a fair account. (laughs)

Mark: So, what happened to the government after two years? In my book *Anwar Returns*, I warned that disunity is death. What I meant was that it was so important for everyone to be united in terms of where they were going, and to have objectives and principles they were going to abide by. But it just didn't happen, did it? Was it frustrating for you because you couldn't really change it?

Anwar: They had very minimal influence on Mahathir. He didn't listen.

Mark: He deliberately ignored them?

Anwar: Our friends at the DAP also thought that they could do things, but I told them the Malay reaction is severe. And after that, when the DAP was with us and telling Mahathir that there is this reaction, in every by-election we were smashed. Can you imagine? The only by-election that we won was my constituency, my seat of Port Dickson. I mean, any sensible guy would have some understanding that this was going to happen. They were in a state of denial, I tell you. (taps table repeatedly)

Mark: Yes.

Anwar: And particularly Bersatu, Mahathir's party. Just smashed! That, I think, prompted Muhyiddin to ensure his survival by working with PAS, and by getting people, some in UMNO, to cross over and challenge Pakatan Harapan.

Mark: PAS did well in the election, didn't they?

Anwar: Yes. Before GE15, PAS had 18 parliamentary seats.

Mark: Yes.

Anwar: Now, they're 40, 49.

Mark: Ah ...

Anwar: Yes.

Mark: Not all from Terengganu.

Anwar: No, from Terengganu, Kelantan and all the other states.

PAS is the Malaysian Islamic Party focused on Islamic fundamentalism. It has advocated the long-term goal of creating an Islamic state in Malaysia. From time to time, it has attempted to legislate for such things as *hudud* – an Islamic criminal justice system. When it saw its number of parliamentary seats shrink in the 2013 federal election, it started to reassert its Islamic agenda. It also made a concerted effort to expand its voter base beyond the northern peninsular states. It dominates state assemblies in Kelantan and Terengganu.

In February 2020, the party joined with Bersatu President Muhyiddin Yassin, UMNO leaders and PKR defectors led by Azmin Ali at the Sheraton Petaling Jaya Hotel in an attempt to change the government.

WHY DID PAKATAN HARAPAN COLLAPSE?

Mark: Now, why do you think the government fell when it did?

Anwar: In the 22 months?

Mark: Yes.

Anwar: I think we alienated the Malay base completely and we suffered in the process. The Malay base, yes. That's why PAS is now getting very agitated. They are furiously attacking anything I say. Saying I'm too liberal, too pro-America. Now, when we release President Biden's letter, it will be worse. (both laugh)

Mark: But the Malays have always been suspicious of the DAP and your relationship with it?

Anwar: Yes. But then there was an opportunity to correct it, like now, for example. Anthony Loke (Secretary General of DAP), to his credit, he's doing it, so people say: "Oh no, it is a different DAP." When the rulers, when I meet them, they say: "Oh, it's different." And I say: "No, this is the same DAP." Then they say: "No, look he's reasonable, he speaks good Malay." So that helps immensely in changing the perception. And, of course, now we are the government, they couldn't care two hoots about Malay sentiments or Islam. I have to do it. I have to do it because you have to regain the Malay base, but of course we attend the Chinese functions, we attend the Hindu Thaipusam. You cannot assume that they are with you unless you do something meaningful to show that you're fair.

Mark: Do you live at the prime minister's official residence at Putrajaya?

Anwar: I sometimes go and change in the private room. The private room is also a palace. Then you have the main area. I don't know how many group meeting rooms. After Mahathir built it, Najib then made some changes, refurbished it and then Muhyiddin spent RM34 million to refurbish it and get new paint, everything. Too much extravagance and waste.

Mark: You've hit the ground running really, haven't you?

Anwar: Mmm ... immediately.

Mark: How has your appointment been received internationally?

Anwar: The Australian Prime Minister was very kind, very nice.

Mark: My impression after speaking to Chinese and Indian Malaysians is that they are very supportive of you. Is that your feedback?

Anwar: Really?

Mark: I think that was because of the fear of being marginalised further. Things such as the prospect of the introduction of Shariah law was also worrying for them.

Anwar: Yes. Because Muhyiddin in the campaign was very clear that we must secure this as a Malay country and must worry about the fact that there is an effort to Christianise the country, and the Jews have their influence. Can you imagine? From Muhyiddin! Saying these things! And this was just three days before the election. I was really thinking, that's so stupid and I said no. But I saw social media and the response from the Malay base, I was really worried. I told family and friends, I said: "Look, we're in trouble," and they said: "No, no." Yes. I said, even in my constituency, because I moved from Port Dickson to another constituency which is in tough territory. Tough. But I thought I could make it. But three days before that, my political secretary, Farhash, who was direct with me, said: "Look, you're in trouble. The Malay base, you've got to go and meet them." I said: "No, I can't travel all over", but I did.

Mark: What reaction did you get?

Anwar: When I went there, I remember at prayers they said to me: "No, you're okay, we support you."

PLANS FOR MALAYSIA

Mark: Well, what are your plans for Malaysia, now that you're prime minister?

Anwar: It must be good governance and democratic accountability. That's in terms of governance, but the focus must be on the economy. You see, if we were really determined and effective in cleaning up, in rejecting corruption, we can save billions.

Mark: Well, I read what you said, that Malaysia could become a first world country if it managed to rid itself of corruption.

Anwar: In two months, I've saved RM5 billion. Yes, in two months! From the contracts that I have found. Because there are more, right? I closed this, I jammed this, I renegotiated the tenders. Five billion. It's no joke, in two months.

Mark: Well, that's real money.

Anwar: Yes, it's real money.

THE THREATS: PROTECTIVE SECURITY

Anwar: And then, you know, they'll go after you if you try to stop corruption, that's why you can see the extent of my security. I told the Inspector-General of Police: "You know what, this is embarrassing, with my background, you need to *salaam* everybody, then suddenly you have all these commandos around me." He said: "Please, this is because of the threats."

Mark: Have there been threats?

Anwar: Yes, of course. First, the extremists, Islamic Malays, who are not really violent, but then there are all the tycoons.

Mark: Ah, of course.

Anwar: Yes, it's huge.

Threats come in all ways. On 21 February 2023, security personnel discovered a highly venomous black cobra at the prime minister's house. It was one metre long and weighed about 800 grams. The cobra was spotted near the guard house. It was captured by Malaysian Civil Defence Force officers.

Mark: I wondered why there were about 20 police officers in the hallway.

Anwar: Yes, yes, yes. (laughs)

Mark: Actually, it should be, shouldn't it?

Anwar: In fact, I've complained from the beginning, but they said: "Give it one month, sir, please, security is our forte, we have to, and we know what we're doing …" I said: "Okay." It was the first month gone, and I said: "But still, strict security," … "No, we reduce at the right time, you know," the Inspector-General told me. Yesterday was a meeting with the National Security Council. I said: "You can reduce security now for this meeting."

Mark: Well, that made sense.

Anwar: I told the Inspector-General that I'm going to the mosque today, and that I've got to *salaam* everybody, and can they stay some distance away? He replied: "Okay, we'll try our best, but we cannot reduce the security." Because when you *salaam*, you have everybody around you, which makes it very difficult.

Mark: You have to move around and greet people, don't you?

Anwar: Yes, because I have to do my job. They told me that they will do their job, too. It's embarrassing.

Mark: Hopefully nothing happens.

Anwar: Yes, hopefully, but you feel the need to move amongst the people. There's a time when you know, when you feel you just need to do it. You have waited for so long. You have travelled for so long, to do what? To do it. So do it! That's my point.

Mark: And the thing is, I suppose there's so much to do, isn't there?

Anwar: Yes, there's a lot to do.

Mark: So you're working long hours, quite obviously.

Anwar: I leave the house early in the morning. Sometimes I don't go back to change. I change at the office or the official residence, I go back for the evening functions. There are a lot of meetings. It is quite tiring. People tell me that I need to have a break, at least a day in a week, but I can't with so much to do. In the two months, I took one day off.

Mark: Yes. But I'm sure you just kept working.

Anwar: Yes, I know.

Mark: So, did you spend more time at home then?

The family is very closely knit. Photo from Nurul Izzah's Facebook page.

Anwar: Ah, this is interesting. My grandson, Izzah's son, he said: "*Papa Tok* ..." They call me *Papa Tok*, or Grandpa. He said: "You know, we are so happy that you are Prime Minister." I said: "Oh, thank you." Then he said: "But ..." and I said: "What?" He said: "... how is it that now you are Prime Minister, we can't get to see you?" And he was sad, you know? I was silent. "Yes," my wife said, "ah, now you better plan and give a good answer."

Mark: Well, you recall, the beautiful photograph in my last book of you with your grandson when you were in that prison hospital? Your grandson actually had a tear running down his cheek, which was very touching, but because it was printed in black and white, you can't see it. You can see it in the colour photograph.

Anwar: Yes, yes, yes.

DAUGHTER NURUL IZZAH

Mark: For the same reason, I was also moved by the recent photograph of you and Wan Azizah hugging your daughter, Nurul Izzah.

Anwar: I remember it.

Mark: My condolences for the loss of her baby. She is very brave to publicly talk about it. My publisher was saying it's wonderful that a woman can actually go out and share her experience.

Anwar: Yes, this was after a week or two. Because she was telling me: "You know, how it is so unfair, that women have to endure this and people don't seem to understand."

Mark: Yes.

Anwar: She told me that she wanted to share this. I said if she wanted to share her experience then she should tell what she has had to endure, the sadness of losing the baby and the pain. And she decided to do it.

Mark: I just think the photograph of the three of you hugging each other is very poignant. It wasn't just about the miscarriage, was it? It was about everything, I suppose. She explained how she had been so busy with the election and other responsibilities that the family really hadn't had much time together.

Anwar: Yes. That's true, and she was just so tough in the campaign, that would've affected her, the doctor said. She conceived during the campaign period.

Mark: The women in your family are very determined, aren't they? Is Izzah the toughest in the family?

Anwar: Yes, she is. But, you know, she has been helping me. I've asked her to be around.

Mark: That's important.

Anwar: I mean, there will be some reactions. People attack me, nepotism. Nothing, it's not part of my remuneration, but I needed the contact, the advice and experience handling the papers.

Mark: But it's good that it's a member of family because it's someone you can trust.

Anwar: Yes, that's true.

Anwar was right about the political reaction to the appointment of his daughter as his advisor on economics and finance. Political opponents criticised her appointment, describing it as nepotism and cronyism, despite him saying she was qualified for the position, and she wasn't receiving any remuneration.

Nevertheless, she resigned the position six weeks later, on 12 February 2023, to take up a new role as co-head of the secretariat committee to the finance minister. The committee's chairman, Tan Sri Mohd Hassan Marican, offered her the role.

LEGISLATIVE PROGRAMME

Mark: And so, have you got a legislative programme mapped out? What are the priorities?

Anwar: Yes, in terms of the anti-corruption drive and economy, because we need to be strong.

Mark: I saw this morning's newspaper, *The Star*, saying that inflation is high: that things are costing more in the markets and shops.

Anwar: Although inflation figures, general figures, have gone down slightly for the last month.

STRENGTH OF COALITION

Mark: What are the challenges of holding your coalition together?

Anwar: For now, it's strong. You know why? Because the late entry was Sarawak, and Sarawak is now solid, more solid than even UMNO, with us. Now us, and Sarawak alone, are already the simple majority. And with BN, [the coalition] is quite strong. By the way, President Biden wrote a nice letter to me.

Mark: Ah, nice, but the Americans have always been supportive of you, haven't they? (laughs)

Anwar: And Biden, since he was foreign relations committee chairman, you remember?

Mark: Ah, yes.

Anwar: The strongest statement was from him about my legal troubles and imprisonment.

Mark: Yes.

Anwar: The strongest ever.

Mark: Yes.

Anwar: He was threatening sanctions at that time.

ARRIVAL OF DEPUTY MINISTER RAMKARPAL SINGH

Staff: Sir, your next meeting is with Ramkarpal Singh (Deputy Minister in charge of Law and Institutional Reform; son of Karpal Singh).

Anwar: Okay. Oh, Ramkarpal. Get Ramkarpal to join us for a while. His sister, Sanjeet, came to see me last week, she was very, very emotional. She said: "Anwar, I can't believe it." I said: "What?" She said: "I can't believe it! You are here." She went on, saying: "Because I spent more time waiting for you outside the prison to get inside. So, when I sat outside here, I said, oh my goodness," she said, "my father Karpal would have loved this."

Mark: Karpal was a wonderful man, a great Malaysian patriot and lawyer. He would have loved to see all this happen. I remember Karpal's second sedition trial, when the government was attempting to convict him and disqualify him from parliament. I remember standing beside you and I remarked, "You know, he never smiles," about Lim Kit Siang, who was standing a few metres away.

Anwar: Yes.

Mark: And you turned to Lim Kit Siang and, pointing to me, said: "He says you never smile." And he actually smiled back, but very briefly.

Anwar: (laughs) Oh, you remember that!

Mark: I do. He rarely smiles. That's true.

Anwar: He quickly loses the smile. Come Ram, come. (Ramkarpal enters the PM's office)

Mark: You better tell him that you've just appointed me as Attorney-General. (both laugh)

Ram: When are you starting the job, next week?

Mark: Well, we can't waste any time. Ram, you obviously didn't trust Mahathir. I saw that you quoted from a tweet, saying about him, "a snake sheds its skin, but remains a snake."

Anwar: No, he did at one stage. We all had to, just compromise, because of the decision of the leadership. But Ram was tougher. He was tougher than Gobind (his brother). The toughest was Sangeet.

Ram: Yes, she …

Anwar: Well, she came last week, you know?

Ram: Yes, she told me.

Mark: We're all scared of her. (all laugh)

Anwar: No, you know what Sangeet said? She was apparently quite emotional. Then she said as she was waiting outside, she said: "You know, I had to do this all the time. Every other week in Sungai Buloh Prison, and then suddenly I come here." So, I brought her in front, to my seat there. So she said: "My God, it's just unbelievable." She's very emotional.

Ram: Yes, she gets emotional about this whole becoming PM and all that.

Mark: Well, it's been such an emotional journey for everyone and to end up as prime minster is extraordinary, isn't it?

Ram: You're writing another book, are you?

Anwar: The final chapter.

Ram: Oh, the same book but with a final chapter?

Anwar: No, the final book. No, there are two books. Now's the third one.

Mark: It's actually the fourth book.

Ram: Oh, yes.

Ram: What's the title of the book?

Mark: It's called *Anwar Triumphs*.

Anwar: Oh, styled like using those Triumph motorcycles. (all laugh)

Mark: We should photograph you in some bike "leathers" (what motorcyclists wear for protection).

Ram: Can you put that as the cover? (all laugh)

Anwar: Do they still produce Triumph motorcycles?

Ram: Oh yes, Triumph motorcycles are still manufactured.

Mark: This fourth book completes the quartet. I think it's absolutely necessary because it goes into the universities so that the young people actually know what happened, and also for the general public. It was critical that an accurate, reliable and complete account be told.

Anwar: Yes.

Ram: So now the latest is *Anwar Triumphs* – that's the final one, right?

Anwar: The third book, *Anwar Returns*, was published in 2018, wasn't it?

Mark: Yes, that's right; obviously, so much has happened since then.

Ram: Well, I wasn't surprised, but of course, you know, towards the end, there was a lot of uncertainty.

Mark: Imagine if your father knew about this.

Ram: Oh yes, of course. Huge thing.

Mark: Prime Minister, I see that you and Ram have work to do. I've taken up far too much of your time and, as always, I'm very grateful for your cooperation. Malaysians can be assured that their country is finally in safe hands, and I wish you well in the difficult tasks that await you.

At the launch of the book, *Anwar Returns*, in 2018.

The author in conversation with Anwar and Ramkarpal Singh for this interview.

CHAPTER 2

Return to Power

There were many who doubted Anwar Ibrahim would ever be prime minister of Malaysia. The road to victory was long and difficult. He spent in all about ten or more years of the last 20 years in prison. Much had happened in the past 20 years, but more was to happen before he finally became the tenth prime minister of Malaysia.

Anwar's release from prison and the King's pardon in 2018 brought about much expectation that he would in time take over from Mahathir as prime minister. That, after all, was the agreement between them. He came so close in 2020, but the transition to Anwar and the prospect of reform was dashed by the betrayal of Mahathir and his sympathisers, and the effective restoration of UMNO to power. It's worth recalling the events before and after the GE14 victory.

This book is about those eventful and dramatic four years.

It revisits those earlier events, not only because they put everything that happened after that in context, but also because they make what followed even more remarkable.

The title of this book – *Anwar Triumphs* – is perhaps the final chapter on a remarkable political and personal journey. Who could have ever believed it was possible, as it seemed in the past 20 years or so to be unthinkable?

CHAPTER 3

Anwar's Trials and Ordeals 2012–2015

My previous books documented the dramatic and often sensational twists and turns of Anwar's legal battles, the trials and appeals, and how they played out in the courts; Anwar's release and full royal pardon in 2018; and, in his own words, a "new dawn" for Malaysia.

It is necessary to recall some of the events that resulted in Anwar's conviction and imprisonment on 10 February 2015 by the Federal Court. These legal proceedings were analysed in careful detail in my third book, *Anwar Returns*, which was published in 2018, but some recall of events is important to understand how and why Anwar was convicted, jailed and then unconditionally pardoned by the Yang di-Pertuan Agong.

It also reveals why his conviction and incarceration in 2015 was against the forensic evidence produced at his trial, suggesting that the whole episode was a political conspiracy to keep him out of parliament.

ALLEGATION OF SODOMY 2008

On 28 June 2008, Mohammed Saiful Bukhari Azlan, a former male aide in Anwar Ibrahim's office, filed a police complaint alleging that he had been forcibly sodomised by Anwar Ibrahim in a private condominium at Damansara two days before.

He alleged that on 26 June 2008, he was asked by Anwar to meet him at a private condominium not far from the centre of Kuala Lumpur to discuss work-related matters and deliver documents. He alleged that when he entered the apartment, he was met by Anwar who demanded sex from him and was taken to a bedroom where he said he was sodomised.

Mohd Saiful also claimed that Anwar had sexually assaulted him some eight or nine times against his will over the previous two months. When challenged as to how a 61-year-old man with a bad back could physically overpower a 24-year-old man, he changed his complaint to "homosexual conduct by persuasion".

Anwar was arrested on 16 July 2008 and released the next day. He was formally charged on 6 August 2008 under section 377B of the Malaysian Penal Code, which punishes "carnal intercourse against the order of nature" with "imprisonment for a term which may extend to twenty years, and shall also be liable to whipping". Anwar pleaded not guilty to the charge.

Sodomy was illegal in Malaysia in 2008, and still is, even for consenting adults. Curiously, the act of sodomy under the law includes not only anal penetration but also acts of fellatio or oral sex.

If convicted, Anwar would also have been forced to relinquish his parliamentary seat. Even if he was sentenced to just one day's imprisonment or fined at least RM2,000 (US$600), he would be barred from standing in elections for five years. Supporters believed that banning him from parliament was the sole reason for bringing the charge.

SAIFUL'S MEDICAL EXAMINATION

Before lodging his police complaint, Mohd Saiful went to the private Hospital Pusrawi at Jalan Tun Razak to be medically examined. He told general surgeon Dr Mohamed Osman Abdul Hamid, who examined him, that his anus had been painful for the past few days and that a "plastic" item had been inserted into it.

A proctoscopy examination showed no physical signs of penetration and a normal anus and rectum. After the examination, Mohd Saiful told the doctor that he had been sodomised by a "VIP".[1] Because of the allegation of sodomy, Dr Mohd Osman advised Mohd Saiful to be re-examined at a government hospital, which he did by going to Hospital Kuala Lumpur (HKL).

However, it wasn't until two hours after the first examination, which was strange because HKL was close to Hospital Pusrawi. Apparently, no explanation was ever given for the delay of two hours.

Three specialist doctors examined him that night, but found no evidence of injury. They said there were "... no conclusive clinical findings suggestive of penetration to the anus and no significant defensive wound on the body of the patient."[2]

They took various swabs from Mohd Saiful's body for scientific analysis. These included swabs taken from his tongue, nipples, body, perianal region and genitals. High and low rectal swabs and blood samples were also taken for DNA profiling.

For some reason, the samples did not reach the chemistry laboratory for analysis until two days later, having been in the custody of the police during that time. That delay and the way the samples were stored by the police, in a filing cabinet without any refrigeration, was to be a critical factor focused on by the expert defence witnesses.

The samples were also opened and relabelled by the police officer into whose custody they were given by the doctors. As we shall see, that was also to become a significant issue on appeal.

Later that night, Mohd Saiful lodged a police report.

On 30 June 2008, despite rumours he was soon to be charged with sodomy, Anwar issued a statement insisting he would fight a by-election later that year for the Permatang Pauh parliamentary seat vacated by his wife and PKR President Dr Wan Azizah Wan Ismail and form a new government.

---

1   Refer to *Anwar Returns: The Final Twist* (Marshall Cavendish Editions, 2018), pp 186–187, for the medical notes of 28 June 2008 taken by Dr Mohd Osman of Hospital Pusrawi.
2   Hospital Kuala Lumpur Medical Report, 28 June 2008

ANWAR ARRESTED

At 1 pm on 15 July 2008, a police team stopped Anwar's vehicle along Jalan Segambut and arrested him. Overseeing the arrest was the Inspector-General of Police, Musa Hassan, who had been a key witness for the prosecution of Anwar for sodomy in 1998.

Anwar was kept overnight in a police cell, released the next day and told to report back to the police within 30 days. He was asked to provide a DNA sample, but refused claiming that it could be misused to fake evidence against him, as it had been at his first trial. However, a toothbrush, hand towel and water bottle, which Anwar had used that night, were seized by the police.

It was later suggested that his DNA had been extracted from these items. The Prosecution would argue that these items would link Anwar to traces of semen found on Mohd Saiful when he was physically examined and samples taken from him. The trial judge excluded evidence obtained in this way as he regarded it unfair that Anwar had not been informed of its possible use against him.

The Prosecution chose to charge Anwar only with the last act allegedly committed at the Desa Damansara Condominium on 26 June, but not the other allegations Saiful had made against his former employer. Anwar was charged with a single offence of sodomy contrary to section 377B of the Penal Code. He pleaded not guilty and was released on bail to later stand trial.

POLITICAL CONSPIRACY?

After his release, Anwar said that the allegation was a high-level conspiracy to prevent him from entering Parliament, adding that he had refused to give his DNA as he did not believe in the system, saying "It should not be used as a personal vendetta against me. I was questioned for 5½ hours, I was stripped naked including the examination of my private parts. Why treat me like a major criminal and a public enemy?"[3]

Anwar added that Musa Hassan harboured a grudge against him for lodging a report on 1 July 2008 with the Malaysian Anti-Corruption Commission saying that the police chief had fabricated evidence against him in the investigation into the beating he suffered while in police custody ten years earlier.[4]

Anwar's claim of corruption was later corroborated by a former police officer who had led the investigation into the "black eye" injuries inflicted on Anwar when in custody by police chief Rahim Noor in 1998, who later pleaded guilty to the assault when charged.

On 12 September 2011, former city criminal investigation chief, Mat Zain Ibrahim, claimed in an open letter to the then Inspector-General of Police, Bakri Omar, that Musa, who was at the time assistant criminal investigation chief and under the direction of the then prosecuting officer (former Attorney-General) Tan Sri Gani Patail, had in 1998 fabricated evidence against Anwar by stealing his DNA to ensure he would be convicted of sodomy.[5]

With Anwar making a political comeback, many of his supporters viewed the fresh sodomy charge as a desperate attempt by the government to cling to power. The timing of the charge, they suggested, was just too coincidental with his return to politics.

There was some basis for the allegation of a political conspiracy. It came about when Mohd Saiful testified at the trial, which began some 17 months later on 3 February 2010.

He revealed that several days before the alleged sexual assault on 26 June 2008, he had met with then Deputy Prime Minister Najib Razak and a senior police officer, Senior Assistant Commissioner Mohd Rodwan

---

3   ITN Source, 17 July 2008
4   Reuters, 17 July 2008
5   Shannon Teoh, "Mat Zain: Musa, Gani duped Dr M into sacking Anwar"
    themalaysianinsider.com, 12 September 2011

Mohd Yusof. This confirmed what the Defence had suspected all along, that Mohd Saiful was somehow connected to Najib.

Soon after Anwar's arrest, Najib Razak told reporters that he was not involved in the case at all and denied knowing Mohd Saiful. But when the opposition alliance produced a photograph showing the complainant with a staff member at the DPM's office, he said that the photograph was taken three months earlier when Mohd Saiful visited his office to apply for a government scholarship.[6]

Three days later, however, Najib admitted that several days before the alleged incident, Mohd Saiful had in fact met with him at his residence, at which time he revealed he had been sodomised by Anwar. At a press conference held at his parliament office, the then DPM said: "I received his visit in my capacity as a leader and he as an ordinary citizen who wanted to tell me something ... I don't (sic) know him before this."[7]

Najib denied he had advised Mohd Saiful to lodge a police report.

It further emerged that the day before the alleged incident with Anwar, Mohd Saiful met with Senior Assistant Police Commissioner Mohd Rodwan in Room 619 of the Concorde Hotel in Kuala Lumpur.

Mohd Rodwan had played a key role in the police team in Anwar's earlier trials in 1998. He is particularly remembered for allegations against him of illegally using Anwar's blood sample for DNA testing and allegations of planting fabricated DNA samples on the mattress brought to court, which police alleged was where the sexual act took place.

When asked about the meeting with Saiful, Mohd Rodwan refused to comment to the media. Anwar's supporters saw his involvement as further evidence of a conspiracy to discredit the opposition leader.

Anwar maintained throughout the proceedings that "... this is a malicious, trumped-up case and shouldn't have started in the first place."[8]

---

6   *The Star*, 30 June 2008
7   Bernama, 3 July 2008
8   Reuters, 26 March 2010

In the weeks leading up to the commencement of the trial in early 2010, Anwar told the media he intended to subpoena Prime Minister Najib and his wife as witnesses at his trial,[9] but the trial judge set aside the witness summons, and they did not testify.

The Defence made several applications to strike out the charge, which included abuse of process given the absence of any physical injuries, failure of the Prosecution to provide full disclosure and asking the trial judge to disqualify himself for actual bias, all of which were rejected by the trial judge.

WAS THE TRIAL FAIR?

There was some suggestion that Anwar did not get a fair trial. Many argue that he couldn't complain given he was acquitted. Lawyers may take a different view, as that question cannot be judged simply on the final result.

As a lawyer, I concluded that some of the trial judge's rulings were questionable, but in other respects he was limited by the legal procedure that operates in Malaysia, and yet some of these matters were fully in his discretion to decide.

There were aspects that were concerning, which included failure of the Prosecution to properly disclose material, such as witness statements, a prosecution list of witnesses to be called, and the material on which expert reports were based. That would not happen in some other countries, where the law has developed in favour of full disclosure as a matter of fairness to accused persons.

The medical reports detailing the physical examination of the complainant and DNA reports were disclosed to the Defence pursuant to section 51A of the Criminal Procedure Code (CPC). However, access was denied to the materials on which the reports were based. The Prosecution refused to disclose Mohd Saiful's hospital records, which Anwar's lawyer, Karpal Singh, submitted was material that should be disclosed.

---

9   *New Straits Times*, 3 February 2010

Before cross-examining Dr Razali, who was one of the three doctors at HKL to medically examine Saiful on the night of 28 June 2008, Karpal Singh applied to inspect the complete history of the medical examination, including any clinical notes, reports and specimens taken by the examining doctors, as well as their qualifications and medical experience.

In particular, he wanted access to the primary hospital notes recorded during Mohd Saiful's examination. He had seen a composite medical report dated 13 July 2009, but not the notes on which it was based (called at trial the "proforma notes").

He told the court that the proforma notes were critical in assessing Dr Razali's credibility, particularly if there were contradictions between his testimony and Mohd Saiful's recorded medical history. He maintained this was "more than a hunch".

Finally, he submitted that since Dr Razali was giving expert testimony, any material which formed the basis of his opinion should be disclosed to the Defence. He accepted that it was not automatically admissible into evidence, but that the court could call for its production so that it may be tested under cross-examination.

The trial judge, Justice Zabidin, agreed with the Prosecution, which opposed disclosing the material and ruled that he would not order the Prosecution to produce the proforma notes to the Defence, although he did accept that the Defence would be entitled to see the notes if the witness referred to them, but at that stage he had not done so.

The law requires that should any witness refresh his or her memory from a document when testifying, the document must be produced to the other party to enable it to cross-examine the witness if it chooses.

Karpal commenced to cross-examine Dr Razali, during which the doctor admitted that he could not remember everything that transpired during the three-hour examination. He was repeatedly asked if he wanted to refer to the notes made at the time of the examination, but on each occasion, he declined to do so.

It was obvious that Karpal was attempting to trap the witness into using the notes to refresh his memory. If the witness referred to them for that purpose, Karpal could then compel the document to be produced. Dr Razali was too cagey to fall for that trick, saying he just could not remember the details.

The next morning, Karpal renewed his application for the disclosure of the material on the basis that the doctor was deliberately being evasive, but the judge held firm on his ruling not to grant access to the proforma notes.

Anwar with Karpal Singh.

"PILLOW TALK"

While the fight for disclosure of Mohd Saiful's medical records was being waged with the doctors who had examined him at HKL, the hearing was interrupted by an extraordinary revelation – that Mohd Saiful was having an affair with a female member of the Prosecution team. It raised the question of whether the prosecution should be discontinued.

The allegation had first surfaced in late July 2010, when fugitive blogger Raja Petra Kamarudin alleged in his blog, *Malaysia-Today*, that Junior Deputy Public Prosecutor Farah Azlina Latif, who was part of an eight-person Prosecution team, was having an affair with Mohd Saiful.

The Attorney-General Abdul Gani Patail reacted immediately and removed Farah Azlina from the trial team. In doing so, he made no admission that there was any truth in the allegation, saying:[10]

> The Attorney-General's Chambers cannot compromise on any issue that can tarnish the image or credibility of the department and we are looking at such matters very seriously. This can be very difficult for us but any personal matter, if it can have any implication in whatever form on the department, will be handled very seriously.

Abdul Gani told the media at a press conference at his office that Farah Azlina had to be dropped, not because she was found guilty, but to avoid any negative public perception of the Prosecution team. "This move is also to ensure that the smooth running of the case is not affected," he said.

He also added that Farah Azlina had very limited involvement in the case, pointing out that she only assisted in recording all notes on the proceedings. "She had no access at all to the investigation papers or any confidential information that the prosecution has."[11]

Farah Azlina may well have been a junior prosecution lawyer with limited involvement in the conduct and planning of the trial, but it tainted

---

10   The Associated Press, 27 July 2010
11   *The Star*, 28 July 2010

the entire case. She was intimately involved with the complainant in a prosecution, which depended on his credibility.

How could his word be relied upon when he had a direct link to the Prosecution? It opened the prospect that he could have been told things he should not have known, or seen documents and exhibits, which in turn might have influenced his testimony.

There were other factors that emphasised the seriousness of the affair and its potential to compromise the trial. The Prosecution didn't deny the affair. Junior prosecutor or not, Farah Azlina had direct access to prosecution material. How was she able to develop a romantic relationship during the trial? It had to be assumed that, unless they already knew each other, there was frequent contact between them to enable a relationship to develop. But that hardly seemed likely if she was no more than a mere "note-taker" at the trial. She must have had direct access to him during the trial or after hours, or both.

During that interaction, there was every prospect that there was indiscreet talk about the trial, including what he was going to say – or what would be called "pillow talk". They may have discussed nothing of consequence, but critically, the opportunity was there to do so. That situation should never have occurred.

Farah Azlina's relationship with Mohd Saiful completely compromised the prosecution case. Dropping her from the Prosecution team did not solve the problem because the perception that the prosecution case had been compromised by the affair was inescapable. It is a fundamental principle of natural justice that the mere appearance of bias is sufficient to overturn a judicial decision. It prompts the oft-quoted aphorism: "Not only must justice be done; it must also be seen to be done".

The Prosecution should always be a "model litigant" and above suspicion. It must not be seen to have acted in any way that might suggest it has acted improperly or inappropriately.

For that reason alone, the trial should have been abandoned. The trial judge couldn't order that to happen, as it was up to the Attorney-General to make that decision. He would also have to decide whether it was appropriate to charge the person again and appoint a new Prosecution team to take the matter to trial.

The Defence applied to strike out the charge on the basis that the prosecution had been compromised. Anwar's lawyer, Karpal Singh, said that following the revelation of the affair between Saiful and Azlina, "the entire Prosecution team should step down." The chief prosecutor, Mohd Yusof, brushed the complaint aside, saying in response that the affair was "mere allegations without any substance."

The application by the Defence to strike out the sodomy charge was refused by the trial judge. An application to stay the proceedings pending an appeal of the trial judge's dismissal of the application was made. Initially, the trial judge just refused to adjourn, but later changed his mind. The appeal was ultimately unsuccessful, and the trial continued on in the Courts Complex off Jalan Duta.

THE JUDGE'S VERDICT OF ACQUITTAL

The trial continued on for some months, with many interruptions, all of which were detailed in my earlier book, *Anwar Returns*, but it finally concluded and Judge Zabidin set a date for the delivery of his decision. It was to be held on 9 January 2012.

The opposition alliance, Pakatan Rakyat (PR), had promised to gather a 100,000-strong crowd outside the court building on Jalan Duta as a show of support for Anwar.

At first, the police were firmly of the view that no demonstration would be allowed to take place. Rally organisers then met with senior police, including Kuala Lumpur police chief Datuk Mohmad Salleh. It was agreed that a rally could take place at the court complex, but that the crowd would be confined to a car park and limited to no more than 5,000 supporters.

The police later claimed that representatives of Parti Keadilan Rakyat (PKR), the political party of which Anwar was *de facto* head – including PKR Youth chief Shamsul Iskandar Mohd Akin, PKR strategic director Rafizi Ramli, Wanita chief Zuraida Kamaruddin and vice-president N. Surendran – had signed an agreement to abide by ten conditions in holding the rally.

The representatives, however, disputed that there had been such an agreement, even though the police were able to produce a document that apparently had been signed by them.

The rally was authorised under section 27 of the Police Act. The conditions, which the police claimed were agreed to by PKR representatives, included the prohibition of brochures and banners with the tagline "*Bebaskan Anwar*" ("Free Anwar") in any circumstances during the rally. Public speaking and loudhailers were not allowed, and protesters were to gather only in the area marked by the police line.

On the morning of 9 January 2012, when I arrived at the High Court Complex, the police were strictly controlling crowd access to the area. Supporters were being held back by police officers stationed at nearby road junctions. At about 8.30 am, a crowd of about 5,000 or so had been admitted to the large car park designated for the gathering of supporters.

Despite the prohibition of banners and placards, many of the supporters held them with slogans of "Free Anwar" and "Free Anwar 901". The police did nothing to remove them. The crowd was noisy, but orderly. The police presence was obvious, but they simply surrounded the court and kept the crowd in check.

At about 8.45 am, Anwar arrived at the court complex and, with his family, walked the 200 metres or so up the main driveway surrounded by chanting supporters. After passing through the main security gates at the end of the main driveway, he made his way through the assembled media to enter the building. Once through the main doors, Anwar walked past a cordon of police and took the lift to Judge Zabidin's courtroom on the fifth floor.

The courtroom in which the trial took place was relatively small. The public gallery consisted of five rows of bench-seats that could accommodate about 50 people. The courtroom was full of family members, supporters, foreign embassy representatives, and local and international media.

Seating was at a premium that morning – all seats were taken, and many had to stand. The benches set aside for lawyers were full of counsel from the Defence and Prosecution.

With Judge Zabidin's permission, I had throughout the trial been seated in a side-bench usually reserved for the media. That morning, there were others sitting beside me. They included the investigating police officer, DSP Jude Pereira, who had played a prominent and controversial role in the investigation. Also seated at the bench was a lawyer holding a "watching brief" for Mohd Saiful and who had been present during most of the trial. I had no idea why the lawyer was there or what he was expected to do on Saiful's behalf, given that Saiful was a prosecution witness.

COURTROOM DECISION

Court was due to start at 9 am but, as usual, there were delays. It took time for the public gallery to settle. The lawyers entered the court at different times. Karpal Singh characteristically arrived late.

Minutes later, the buzzer sounded to announce the judge's entry and the police usher called out "all rise", announcing the arrival of the judge and declaring that the court was in session. Judge Zabidin quickly slipped into his seat without looking at anyone and immediately began to read his decision. It took no more than a matter of minutes. He said:[12]

---

12 Author's notes and as reported in major news publications

Elation after the verdict of acquittal for Anwar, his wife and the family.

> After going through the evidence, the court could not with 100 per cent certainty exclude the possibility that the [DNA] sample is not compromised, and finds that it is not safe to rely on the sample. As such, the court is left only with Saiful's testimony. As this is a sexual crime, the court is always reluctant to convict based entirely on Saiful's testimony, which is uncorroborated. The accused is thus acquitted and discharged.

Judge Zabidin's decision was greeted with sighs of relief and cheers from the gallery, and with that he got up and quickly left the courtroom. Understandably, Anwar's family was delighted, if not a little shocked by the verdict of acquittal. It was a very emotional and tearful moment for them, as they hugged each other and their supporters. Anwar's wife, Wan Azizah Wan Ismail, was tearful and exhausted as she threw her arms around her husband.

Anwar, with his family and supporters, left the courtroom and walked out through the main doors of the building to be confronted by a swarm of television cameras. News of his acquittal had spread quickly to the crowd gathered outside and he was greeted with cheers and the chant of *"Reformasi, Reformasi"* ("Reform") from the crowd behind the main gates 50 metres away.

Anwar declared to the media that he was surprised and vindicated by the decision. He then walked to the crowd of supporters and, with his wife and daughters by his side, addressed them using a loudhailer.

Shortly after, Melissa Goh of Channel NewsAsia interviewed Anwar. When asked about the trial, he replied: "This was a farcical trial, a travesty of justice. So, a decision to the contrary would have put Malaysia in a disastrous light. That I know for a fact. UMNO had made a decision that Anwar was guilty."

"Why the sudden change of mind then?" asked Ms Goh.

Anwar meets members of the media.

"Because," Anwar replied, "they [the government] also understand the anger, the public outrage here, and international repercussions."

Loud explosions suddenly interrupted the interview. Anwar's daughters, who were standing behind him, urged him to leave and he quickly left the area. Police dispersed the crowd and declared the area to be unsafe.

They found explosive devices under police traffic cones. That day, five people were injured and several cars damaged. Kuala Lumpur police chief Datuk Seri Mohmad Salleh later said that homemade explosives were used. Investigators said they found battery remnants, pieces of wire, ball bearings and timers.

PM NAJIB'S REACTION TO ACQUITTAL

Prime Minister Najib said that the verdict showed "once again that, despite what many have claimed, the Malaysian judiciary is independent." He said it was an institution where neither politics nor politicians had any influence over the dispensation of justice. This, he said, strengthened the clear separation of powers of each branch of the government with neither of the branches interfering with the workings of the other.

He further said that:[13]

> As head of the executive branch, I respect the decisions of the other branch of government – the judiciary. This case was brought by a private individual and it was important that he had his accusations heard in court. Far from being a politically motivated prosecution, it has been an unwelcome distraction from the serious business of running our country in the interests of the Malaysian people.

He added that the ruling meant the government had been cleared once and for all of the many baseless accusations of political interference and conspiracy against the opposition leader.

13 *New Straits Times*, 10 January 2010

TRIAL JUDGE'S REASONS FOR ACQUITTAL

Judge Zabidin took immediate leave after delivering his verdict. It was only six months later, on 8 July 2012, that he delivered written reasons for acquitting Anwar.

In his written reasons, Judge Zabidin said that one critical ingredient of the charge which needed to be proved was the fact of anal penetration. The three doctors who examined Mohd Saiful at HKL believed that penetration had occurred because government chemist Dr Siew Sheue Feng said he had found semen, which he called "Male Y", from which he extracted DNA that matched Anwar's profile. The judge accepted that corroboration of the fact of penetration from these witnesses "hinged" on Dr Siew's analysis.

However, he was faced with conflicting expert testimony as to whether the DNA actually belonged to Anwar. The government chemist said it was Anwar's DNA, while Anwar's experts said that it would have been impossible to extract any identifiable DNA from the forensic samples.

Justice Zabidin said that to resolve that conflict in the evidence, he needed "to re-evaluate the entire evidence relating to collecting, handling and analysing the samples taken from the complainant, in the light of the defence evidence to see whether the prosecution had proven its case beyond reasonable doubt."

Ultimately, he found he could not exclude the possibility that the integrity of the samples had been compromised before they reached the laboratory for DNA analysis. As such, he could not be satisfied this evidence was capable of corroborating the fact of penetration.

That left him only with the evidence of the complainant who he had found to be a truthful and reliable witness when considering the case to answer submission. He said that although it was open to him to convict on that evidence alone, he was not prepared to do so in the circumstances. The judge expressed it in these terms:[14]

---

14 "Judge's Reasons for Decision", published 8 July 2012, paras 205–207

It was the prosecution stance that the tampering with P27 [plastic exhibit bags containing forensic samples] did not in any way compromise the integrity of the samples in the receptacles since the receptacles were individually sealed with Hospital Kuala Lumpur seal. DW3 [Professor David Wells] when examined on this subject said that the receptacles were not tamperproof [meaning the seal could be removed and resealed] from the manner in which they were sealed and the type of material used as seals. By cutting open P27, the confidence in the integrity of the samples was gone.

After going through the defence's evidence particularly those stated above, this court could not, at this stage, with 100 per cent certainty, exclude the possibility the integrity of the samples taken from the complainant had been compromised before they reached PW5 [Dr Siew Sheue Feng] for analysis. As such, it was not safe to rely on the DNA result obtained by PW5 from the analysis conducted on those samples. That being the case, there was no evidence to corroborate the evidence of PW1 [Mohd Saiful] on factum of penetration.

Judge Zabidin was left to conclude as follows:

This court was left only with the evidence of PW1 to prove penetration. This being a sexual offence, it is trite law that the court is always reluctant to convict an accused person based solely on the uncorroborated evidence of the complainant. Therefore, the accused is acquitted and discharged from the charge.

AUTHOR'S OBSERVATIONS

It may assist the reader for me to set out my own observations on the basis for the trial judge's verdict to acquit. They are twofold. First, the integrity of the DNA evidence. Secondly, what to make of the uncorroborated testimony of Mohd Saiful.

DNA EVIDENCE

Judge Zabidin, in his reasons for acquittal, relied on the observation of defence expert witness Professor David Wells that the plastic exhibit bags, which contained the forensic samples, were not tamperproof. He said he could not be satisfied the integrity of the forensic samples had not been compromised before they reached Dr Siew Sheue Feng for analysis because the plastic bags had been opened by the police.

The defence expert witnesses had been highly critical of Detective Superintendent Jude Pereira's management of the forensic samples that were obtained by the HKL doctors from their medical examination of the complainant.

The samples had been placed into airtight containers and then sealed in plastic exhibit bags. The exhibit bags were then labelled and given to Pereira to deliver to the government chemist for analysis. Pereira admitted during his testimony that he had opened the exhibit bags before delivering them to the laboratory for analysis and then, contrary to explicit instructions, had stored them in a filing cabinet in his office for 43 hours instead of in a freezer.

The defence expert witnesses were also critical of what happened to the samples when they arrived at the government laboratory. Dr Seah Lay Hong, who received the samples for analysis, also broke the essential chain of custody by ignoring the labelling given to each of them by the examining doctors and relabelling each with her own description. It meant that there was no proven continuity between the samples taken by the doctors and the samples analysed by her.

Chain of custody is critical when forensic evidence is involved. The integrity of forensic samples must be maintained by providing documentation and evidence of the control, transfer and analysis of the samples.

If forensic evidence is to be used in court to convict persons of crimes, it is essential that it must be handled in a scrupulously careful manner to avoid allegations of tampering or misconduct, which can compromise the prosecution case. It requires that evidence be identified as being in substantially the same condition as it was at the time it was seized, and that it has remained in that condition through an unbroken chain of custody.

Judge Zabidin did not need to go any further than he did in concluding that he could not rely on the integrity of the samples after the chief police investigator had compromised them in the way he did, but arguably the integrity of the samples was further compromised at the laboratory.

UNCORROBORATED TESTIMONY OF COMPLAINANT

Judge Zabidin, in his reasons for acquittal, concluded that he could not exclude the possibility that the integrity of the forensic samples had been compromised. That conclusion meant that he could not rely on that evidence to corroborate the complainant's allegation of sexual assault. It left him only with the uncorroborated evidence of Mohd Saiful to prove penetration. Something needs to be said about that.

The need for corroboration of a complainant's evidence in a sexual offence case is well settled at law. Whilst there is no rule of law in Malaysia (as in many other countries) that a complainant's evidence must be corroborated, it is accepted that it would be unsafe to convict in cases of this kind unless the complainant's evidence is unusually convincing or there is some corroboration of the complainant's story.

It is accepted by Malaysian courts that allegations of sodomy can easily be made and be very difficult to refute, and that the evidence in support of such a charge has to be very convincing in order to convict the accused.

A trial judge hearing such a case must warn himself or herself that it is dangerous to convict without corroboration. For a discussion of this principle, see the judgement of the Court of Appeal in *Datuk Seri*

Anwar bin Ibrahim v Pendakwa Raya [2004] 1 MLJ 177, where the court at Anwar's first appeal dealt with a claim that there was no corroboration of the complainant's allegation. Without any DNA evidence, there was no independent evidence to support the complainant's allegation of sodomy.

Mohd Saiful's complaint of sexual assault to the medical doctors who examined him on the night of 26 June 2008 was not corroborative evidence. The fact that he said he had been sodomised could not prove that his claim was true. In his reasons for refusing the no case submission at the close of the Prosecution's case, the trial judge incorrectly said it did. When he delivered his verdict, he properly took a different view.

Of course, evidence of injury isn't necessary to prove penetration, but it makes it more likely. There was no medical evidence of injury of the complainant's anus or rectum consistent with penile penetration that might have corroborated his allegation.

In these circumstances, Judge Zabidin was not prepared to convict based solely on Mohd Saiful's uncorroborated testimony. No complaint can be made of that decision as it was consistent with the facts and in accordance with established legal principles.

PROSECUTION'S APPEAL AGAINST ANWAR'S ACQUITTAL

Section 50(3) of the Courts of Judicature Act 1964 provides that a criminal appeal to the Court of Appeal from a trial in the High Court "may lie on a question of fact or a question of law or on a question of mixed fact and law".

An appeal court may review all of the evidence admitted at trial to determine whether the judge has correctly acquitted an accused. The prescribed time for parties to lodge an appeal in Malaysia is 14 days from the date of the verdict.

Malaysian law allows parties to file only a notice of intention to appeal without providing grounds, which is what the Prosecution did in this case. Grounds of appeal can be filed later.

On the afternoon of Friday, 20 January 2012, the Attorney-General's Chambers (AGC) filed a notice of appeal against the trial judge's verdict of acquittal. The decision to appeal was consistent with the uncompromising approach taken by the Attorney-General in prosecuting this case, and it was not unexpected, particularly when it was reported that Deputy Prosecutor Mohd Yusof had recommended it.

The AGC issued a statement saying:[15]

> The victim's family has urged for an appeal to be filed against the said decision whilst the Malaysian Bar Council has given an opposing view. In this regard, to be fair to the parties concerned, especially the victim and Anwar Ibrahim, the Attorney-General's Chambers wishes to emphasise that in making any decision, the department acts solely on the evidence and in accordance with the law, not influenced by any emotion or parties.

The Prosecution was obviously keen to point out that its decision was not influenced by the views of interested parties, but was based "solely on the evidence and in accordance with the law." Nevertheless, it is interesting to note that the Prosecution was still referring to Mohd Saiful as the "victim", which was plainly inconsistent with the judge's verdict.

Anwar's lawyer, Sankara Nair, had not formally received the notice of appeal when the media told him that it had been filed. His immediate response was:[16]

> However, if it is true, then it is most regrettable and atrocious given that the trial judge has stated succinctly, in his verdict, that the crucial evidence was tampered with. Hence the substratum of the prosecution case is fatally demolished, rendering any appeal,

---

15   Reuters, 20 January 2012
16   *The New York Times – Asia Pacific*, 21 January 2012

no matter how many times, a desperate act of futility. It appears to be a case of political persecution of Anwar and not prosecution.

The Prosecution undoubtedly filed the notice of appeal to comply with the 14-day time limit imposed by legislation and to enable the AGC to obtain a copy of the trial judge's written reasons for his decision, without which it would be difficult to frame the grounds of appeal. It may also be that the Prosecution had already decided, even without those reasons, to appeal because of the view it took of the evidence at the trial.

COURT OF APPEAL

The High Court acquitted Anwar on 9 January 2012, but the Prosecution immediately appealed the decision, which would ultimately be heard before the Malaysian Court of Appeal.

The title of my last book included the phrase "The Final Twist". It was meant to explain the way Anwar Ibrahim was dealt with in the criminal justice system. While all of the trappings of justice were there in the courtroom, what happened was a process contrived to convict him.

When Anwar alleged "political conspiracy", it wasn't just a hollow claim unconnected to the evidence. It had every appearance of being an attempt to once and for all remove him from politics.

The pivotal moment was the case management hearing at the Istana Kehakiman (Palace of Justice) in Putrajaya on the morning of 28 February 2014. It changed everything. That was when it became obvious what was actually "in play", meaning the plan of action against him.

With multiple legal applications yet to be decided, the judge listed the appeal for hearing before the Court of Appeal less than a week away.

The applications were all listed to be heard in the week before the hearing, one of which was listed to be heard at 4.30 pm, which is when the court usually finishes for the day. The court reserved none of its judgements, which were delivered orally. Anwar lost all the applications. It cleared the decks for the appeal to be heard on 6 and 7 March 2014.

Anwar's lawyer, Karpal Singh, claimed that he was ambushed at that case management hearing. It pushed Anwar's appeal into a timetable that effectively condensed everything into the space of one week. Karpal concluded that the only possible explanation was that it was part of a political agenda to resolve everything before the by-election for the parliamentary seat of Kajang, for which Anwar had announced he intended to stand as a candidate. If he was convicted, he would not have been able to stand for election.

The appeal hearing was also rushed. The court delivered its oral judgement at 6 pm on Friday, 7 March 2014.

It was a Friday and, rather than adjourn the hearing for sentencing to another date, which would have been a sensible thing to do, the Defence was told that it would happen immediately.

Anwar described the proceeding as a "travesty of justice which had been choreographed." It had every appearance of just that. In the space of one week, the opposition parties effectively lost two of their most senior members, which Karpal believed was always the intention.

The key to Anwar's prosecution was the DNA evidence, which the Prosecution claimed was Anwar's that was detected in samples taken by government doctors from the complainant's rectum some days after the alleged incident. To recall, the Defence experts had concluded that although the DNA produced was that of Anwar Ibrahim, it was clear to them that it was not extracted from the samples taken from Saiful.

Their considered opinion was that:

1. There was evidence of an unidentified third person in the high rectal swabs that had not been explained, which meant that Mohd Saiful had either been penetrated to ejaculation by another male or someone had contaminated the sample by handling it.

2. The DNA analysis was inconsistent with the known history of the samples, meaning there was little, if any, evidence of degradation in circumstances where, contrary to specific instructions, the samples had not been properly preserved by Detective Superintendent Pereira, who had taken the samples into custody.

3. The DNA allegedly taken from sperm cells had survived for more than 96 hours from the time of ejaculation to analysis, which was highly improbable according to scientific experience. It should have degraded significantly, but the government sample was "pristine".

4. The Differential Extraction Process (DEP), used to separate sperm cells from non-sperm cells, was incomplete, admitting the possibility that the DNA claimed to match Anwar's did not come from semen, but rather from non-sperm cells.

Incredibly, this evidence was brushed aside. The court's decision was hurried and superficial. The Defence experts were critical to the final issue of guilt because if what they said was accepted, even to a limited extent, it was sufficient to raise a reasonable doubt in the Prosecution's case.

Justice Dato' Sri Balia Yusof bin Haji Wahi (Balia), who was leading the Court of Appeal, dealt with none of these issues in his remarks. He said that there was "no reason for the learned trial judge to depart from his earlier findings concerning the findings and experience of the Prosecution experts." He was referring to the judge's reasons at the end of the Prosecution's case. He went on to say "... the judge erred in giving weight to the Defence experts who were no more than armchair experts." It was not enough for the judges simply to brush aside the Defence experts, each of whom had significant credentials and experience, in such a parochial and disparaging manner.

Justice Balia concluded his remarks by saying that the Prosecution's appeal was upheld, and that Anwar was accordingly guilty of the offence of sodomy as charged.

It was then about 6 pm and Justice Balia said that he would give Karpal Singh one hour to prepare mitigation of sentence, to which Karpal replied that one hour was simply "unreasonable" and asked him why they were rushing? The judges did not respond but simply got up and left the court to the jeers and boos of the gallery.

At 6.50 pm, the judges returned. There followed a heated and animated exchange between Justice Balia, Karpal and prosecutor Shafee Abdullah.

Shafee was a private lawyer, not from the prosecution service, but who had been appointed to prosecute the case against Anwar by the Attorney-General. If you remember, Shafee had "coincidentally" been present at Najib Razak's house (then deputy prime minister) when Mohd Saiful turned up, only days before the alleged offence occurred.

Karpal again asked for an adjournment so that he might obtain a medical report concerning Anwar's heart and blood pressure. It was a reasonable request, given that Anwar was facing a significant term of imprisonment and the delay being asked for was only one week. The response, however, was bizarre.

Shafee Abdullah suggested that Karpal summarise his client's medical condition. Justice Balia agreed with the prosecutor that a summary would be sufficient for the purposes of sentencing. But Karpal shot back saying he would not be able to effectively submit a proper plea in mitigation without a medical report, which would be a significant factor in the mitigation of sentence. This exchange then followed:

Karpal: Is Your Lordship saying that medical report is not necessary?

Justice Balia: We shall take your word and account of Anwar's ailment. It is our view that you can proceed without a medical report and in that case we shall take it for what it is worth.

Shafee Abdullah: We are not challenging the medical condition.

Karpal: Not challenging what? What is the difference between this case and others? Your Lordship has been at the Bar and you know this is not reasonable.

Justice Balia: Proceed.

At this, the gallery roared in disapproval.

While this was taking place, Anwar's supporters, who had assembled at the rear entrance to the building, could be heard shouting in unison: "Free, free, free Anwar", "*Reformasi*" and "Down with Najib".

In my third book, *Anwar Returns*, which covered these legal wranglings, I observed that Malaysia had every right to be respected for its economic progress and parliamentary system. However, what took place at the Court of Appeal in that single week in March 2014 was nothing short of alarming. Anwar described it as a "travesty of justice". Many thought it was just that.

A modern democratic nation is judged by how it administers its justice system and whether it abides by the principles of the rule of law.

The judges of the Court of Appeal spent much time in their judgement criticising the Defence for what it described as delaying tactics. Whether that was true or not, it was not relevant to the substantive issues for appeal, but was used as some justification of why the court had rushed the appeal process.

While it may be that, to some extent, Anwar's lawyers – as claimed by the Prosecution and court – delayed the proceedings, it was only because Anwar was exercising his rights as an accused under threat of prosecution for an offence carrying a 20-year sentence.

But that is not the issue. Of concern was the unnecessary haste in which the Court of Appeal conducted the proceedings. Why the haste?

Anwar's lawyers were given only one week to prepare for the appeal hearing.

Critical applications relating to the fitness of the prosecutor to conduct the appeal and a Prosecution appeal to strike out another appeal against a court ruling were disposed of three days later.

The Federal Court listed an appeal to be heard with an hour's notice, and without documents having been served on the Prosecution. The court hearing the main appeal sat into the early evening on each day of the actual hearing.

Anwar was sentenced to five years' imprisonment at 6.55 pm.

So again, why the rush? Some commentators say it was to prevent Anwar standing for a parliamentary seat, with nominations closing only days away. I don't know about that, but I do know what I saw that week, and it was disturbing for any lawyer to witness.

The government claimed the court had conducted its affairs according to law, but on this occasion, it fell way below the international standards expected of a modern judicial system.

KARPAL'S SEDITION CONVICTION – DISQUALIFIED FROM PARLIAMENT

I mentioned that some commentators saw the rush as a device not only to remove Anwar from the political scene, but also Karpal Singh as well. Karpal had been charged with committing an act of sedition for comments made by him at a press conference at his offices on 6 February 2009 about the actions of the Sultan of Perak, Sultan Azlan Shah.

The Sultan had intervened to remove the Perak Menteri Besar (Chief Minister) after making personal inquiries as to whether the state government still enjoyed a majority in Parliament following declarations by three government members that they had resigned from the ruling party.

Karpal said during the press conference that the Sultan's removal of the Chief Minister, and appointment of another to fill the office, was beyond his constitutional powers and could be questioned in a court of law.

The Prosecution immediately jumped on these remarks and claimed the words had a "seditious tendency" by bringing hatred or contempt or exciting disaffection against the Sultan. Karpal said he was doing no more than offering a legal opinion that the Sultan was subject to the Malaysian Constitution. Karpal was charged under the Sedition Act a few weeks later in March 2009.

The charge was dismissed when tried before the High Court on 11 June 2010. The trial judge ruled that the Prosecution had failed to prove a *prima facie* case against him. The Court of Appeal later reversed the acquittal and the trial was ordered to continue with Karpal required to enter his defence to the charge.[17]

This was the second time that Karpal Singh was charged with an act of sedition, first in January 2000 and again in March 2009. The first charge was withdrawn by the newly appointed Attorney-General Abdul Gani Patail. The second charge would end in conviction.

These charges spanned a turbulent decade in Malaysia's history. Karpal's sedition trials – a decade apart – provide some insight into the means by which the government had, since 1948, used the legislation to stifle free speech and suppress dissent.

The Sedition Act is a relic of British colonial rule. It was enacted in 1948 to deal with a perceived communist insurrection but remained in force after Malaysia attained independence in 1957, having been preserved under Article 162(1) of the Federal Constitution, which kept pre-existing statutes and gave the Malaysian government the power to amend and repeal them.

During the political unrest of 1969, a state of emergency was declared. Not only was Parliament suspended, but the Sedition Act was also

---

17   See *Pendakwa Raya v Karpal Singh a/l Ram Singh* Criminal Appeal No. W-05-233-2010 delivered on 20 January 2012.

amended so as to broaden its scope.[18] Effectively, the Act has over the past 50 years or so been adapted and extended well beyond the intended scope of the original legislators.

The Sedition Act provides that a person can be convicted on the basis that what they said had a "seditious tendency" – which is an extremely vague phrase. It includes any words spoken which would "bring into hatred or contempt or to excite disaffection against" the government or engender "feelings of ill-will and hostility between different races."

It doesn't matter if the words spoken are true or false. The defendant doesn't need to intend that the words spoken will have one of the results identified in the Act. Legislation of this type hardly seems appropriate in a modern democratic nation, which Malaysia claimed to be.

The Pakatan Harapan government campaigned on a platform promising to repeal oppressive laws, including the Sedition Act. The government announced a moratorium in the use of the Act in October 2018, pending its repeal, but it lifted the moratorium a month later, missing the opportunity for promised reform.

The new PN government, through Home Minister Zainuddin, declared that the Act would continue as it was needed to address the spread of false information or communications that threatened public safety.[19]

Many individuals and organisations continued to criticise the use of the Sedition Act, calling for its repeal, or at least the reinstatement of the moratorium.

On 8 September 2021, the International Federation of Journalists called for the government to drop investigations into several activists from a youth coalition (SSR) demonstrating over a cancelled #Lawan protest on 21 August, but nothing was done.[20]

Soon after the election of the new Pakatan Harapan government, a group of ASEAN MPs at a regional conference held in Malaysia called for

---

18   Modification of Laws (Sedition) (Extension and Modification) Order 1969;
     Emergency (Essential Powers) Ordinance No. 45, 1970
19   Article 19, 27 July 2020
20   International Federation of Journalists, 8 September 2021

the repeal of the 1948 Sedition Act and the 1988 Communications and Multimedia Act to protect MPs and human rights defenders.[21]

At the time of writing, neither of these pieces of legislation have been repealed and continue to be in force, but we return to 2012.

Prime Minister Najib Razak announced his intention on 11 July 2012 to repeal the Sedition Act and replace it with a National Harmony Act, which he claimed would balance freedom of expression with the protection of Malaysia's different cultural and religious groups.

At the same time, the Sedition Act continued to be used against opposition members of parliament, academics and student activists to silence dissent. If anything, prosecutions for sedition became more frequent.

Despite Najib's pledge to repeal what he declared to be outdated legislation, the prosecution against Karpal proceeded to his ultimate conviction and sentence on 11 March 2014. It was just three days after Anwar Ibrahim was convicted of the offence of sodomy and sentenced to five years' imprisonment.

Karpal claimed in his final submission to the High Court that the Attorney-General Abdul Gani Patail had been "influenced by irrelevant considerations. There is no basis for him to exercise his discretion to bring prosecution. It is selective prosecution. There has been discrimination against me. The acts and words of the former PM Mahathir in 1993 to clip the wings of the sultans by setting up a 'special court' was unadulterated sedition. No decision was made at that time to prosecute him and others for clear acts of sedition. I suppose there was no one there to skin the cat."

Karpal's sentencing was fixed for 11 March 2014. The hearing became very heated as Gobind Singh, on behalf of his father, and the prosecutor exchanged insults. The prosecutor Noorin Badruddin submitted that the Sultan had been insulted by Karpal's remarks and that a proper sentence "would include imprisonment".

---

21   ASEAN Parliamentarians for Human Rights (APHR), 26 February 2022

As she said this, the gallery erupted, jeering and shouting at her.

Gobind then jumped to his feet, exclaiming: "This nonsense must stop. She is threatening the court that unless it imposes a significant sentence it would send the wrong signal to the Sultan." He kept going, saying: "If only the prosecutor had the same fire in defending the Constitution. Who is going to defend the Constitution if the AG's Chambers doesn't?"

This comment brought cheers of support from the packed gallery, prompting the prosecutor to stand and shout at the judge in order to be heard: "Why is he attacking our Chambers?" Anwar called out: "Because you deserve it."

Gobind was not to be stopped. The atmosphere in the courtroom was more like a political rally. He continued his impassioned remarks, saying: "The people are sick and tired of this selective prosecution. It happens every day. Do not be threatened by the prosecution service that a light sentence would insult the rulers. Where do we go for justice? We have a duty to defend the Constitution and the courts must defend us. It's the law [the Sedition Act], but a terrible law. It is still your role [the judge] to sentence but don't send Karpal Singh to jail for doing his duty."

The judge put up his hand to still the courtroom, which it did. He then quickly announced his decision, convicting Karpal of sedition and imposing a fine of RM4,000. He immediately got up from his chair and exited through the wood-panelled door behind him.

The conviction, sentence and fine (which was over the limit of RM2,000) meant that, subject to appeal, Karpal would have to vacate his parliamentary seat.

Opposition members of parliament and supporters during this time believed that the government resorted to the criminal law to rid the political system of the main opposition players. After what had happened, it seemed they may have been right. And if they were right, then politics finally destroyed the independence and diminished the reputation of the Malaysian judiciary and the prosecution service.

KARPAL SINGH'S TRAGIC DEATH

Karpal was scheduled to argue Anwar's final appeal before the Federal Court, following Anwar's conviction and sentencing, but his sudden death meant that others – including his son Ramkarpal – would have to argue the case.

His sudden death at such a critical time left the ship rudderless as Anwar's lawyers struggled not only to emotionally come to terms with his loss, but also to frame a series of effective arguments to support the appeal. He was, after all, Anwar's fearless champion and it seemed for a time that his shoes could not be filled.

The accident which killed Karpal happened on the North-South Expressway near the town of Gopeng about 20 kilometres south of Ipoh (or about 180 kilometres north of KL) at around 1.10 am on 17 April 2014.

Karpal was travelling to Penang for a court hearing scheduled for later that morning. Karpal's vehicle in which he was travelling was a Toyota Alphard MPV with the private number plate KS9898. The vehicle had been equipped with a mechanism to lift him from his wheelchair into the front passenger seat, which is where he was seated at the time of the collision. Apart from the driver C. Selvam, others in the vehicle included his faithful and long-time assistant Michael Cornelius, his Indonesian maid and his son Ramkarpal.

The Toyota apparently collided with the rear of a slow-moving five-ton lorry carrying steel and cement. The vehicle was badly damaged, its passenger side ripped apart. Karpal died instantly as did Michael Cornelius, who was seated right behind him. While Karpal's domestic helper was seriously injured, Ramkarpal and Selvam escaped with slight injuries.

The lorry driver Abu Mansor Mohd was not injured and tested positive for cannabis use. Police later charged Selvam with dangerous and reckless driving; there was a suggestion that he fell asleep at the wheel.

Karpal was taken to the Kampar Hospital mortuary. The mood was highly emotional as members of his family arrived in the early hours of that morning. His elegant wife, Gurmit Kaur, was inconsolable, asking "why, why!" as her son Gobind escorted her to the mortuary to view the body. It was a question many were to ask.

At a memorial service on 24 April 2014, Anwar told of his last conversation with Karpal on that fateful night. The telephone conversation took place at around 6.30 pm.

Anwar recounted how Karpal was worried about the pending Federal Court appeal saying he was particularly troubled by the "unprecedented speed at which the appeal records were sent to his office." Anwar said Karpal started to sound agitated and worried, but immediately "switched back to his usual cool and confident self, no doubt intending to put me at ease." He said their long chat ended with the words: "Anwar, you carry on. Don't worry. I'll do my best." Those words were still ringing in his ears when several hours later he heard the news of Karpal's death.

The reaction to Karpal's death was swift, with politicians from opposing sides using social media to respond to the news.

PM Najib Razak said on Twitter: "I have just landed at Ankara when I heard the news that YB Karpal Singh died in a road accident. My condolences to the family." His office later issued a statement saying: "I am shocked to hear of Karpal Singh's tragic passing. In a career that spanned five decades, Karpal's abilities made him a formidable opponent. In politics, he was an implacable leader; in law, a committed advocate."

Anwar wrote on his Facebook profile: "We've lost a colleague; an indefatigable fighter for justice; the legendary Karpal Singh! Our sincere condolences to the family. RIP."

Many others expressed their sorrow at his sudden death.

Karpal's funeral was conducted with full state honours on 20 April 2014 in Penang. Tens of thousands of people attended his funeral and chanted prayers as his body, in a casket covered with a tiger skin, was taken to the Batu Gantong crematorium at George Town.

Along the way, stops were made at the Penang High Court, the State Assembly and his former school, St. Xavier's Institution. The cortege had to make several other unscheduled stops as mourners crowded onto the streets to pay their respects. His body was cremated after the family had completed the final rites. His ashes were later scattered into the sea.

There were a series of memorial tributes to the Bukit Gelugor MP. The seventh and last was held on a rainy evening on 5 May 2014 in Penang. Gobind, in an emotional speech to the assembled crowd, spoke of his father's legacy and told them that it was important to remember "how he lived because he was a man who fought for us and this country, believing that this country can change one day ... a Malaysia where all Malaysians are equal and treated fairly by our government. If there was darkness, Karpal was the light."

Gobind continued: "If there was weakness, it was him who gave us strength. But now that he is no longer with us, are we going to back down now because he is no longer with us? Do we stop our fight because he is no longer here with us? Or do we remember the fighting spirit that the Tiger of Jelutong has left behind?"

The crowd roared with approval.

Karpal Singh was truly a significant figure in Malaysia. He was a larger-than-life character not only because of his involvement in politics, but the law. He had appeared as counsel in most of Malaysia's significant cases over the previous 45 years or so, but it was not just the big cases that mattered to him. His reputation for defending the "little man" was well deserved.

For Karpal, there was no question of retirement. In a CNN interview with Talk Asia in 2002, interviewer Lorraine Hahn asked him whether he had considered retirement, and that perhaps it was time to call it quits and hand over the baton to one of his children.

Karpal responded by saying: "I don't think the question of handing over the baton arises actually because a good lawyer dies in the saddle and that's what it will be as far as I am concerned. To keep going, I think a lawyer has to keep going. I have to go on as long as I can mentally and physically do so."

Karpal's life reflects the modern history of Malaysia and the events that have shaped it as a nation since independence more than 66 years ago. Karpal is very much an integral part of that history.

Before he died, Karpal said that when he is no longer here, "100 Karpals would take my place." If that were only true, but he really is irreplaceable.

A few weeks before his death on 17 April 2014, Karpal Singh was sentenced in the High Court of Malaysia for the criminal act of sedition, for having expressed a legal opinion about the constitutional power of the Sultan of Perak over the State Parliament. Had he failed to overturn the conviction on appeal, the conviction and sentence (with its fine of RM4,000) would have disqualified him from the right to sit as a member of parliament. Karpal's conviction happened on 11 March, four days after Anwar's conviction of the offence of sodomy and sentence of five years' imprisonment.

Karpal saw these convictions as a contrived two-pronged attack on the opposition leadership, which effectively removed both of them from the Federal Parliament.

Of course, both appealed the convictions, but only Anwar lived to challenge his conviction and sentence. Not only did Anwar have to challenge his conviction and sentence, but he also had to face a prosecution appeal to increase what it claimed was a lenient sentence of five years in prison.

The author with Karpal in his office in 2002. Mark Trowell observed both of Karpal's sedition trials in 2002 and 2012.

APPOINTMENT OF DATUK SERI GOPAL SRI RAM
AS LEAD COUNSEL

Originally, senior lawyer Sulaiman Abdullah was to lead Anwar's team at his appeal. However, it became increasingly obvious that his health had not improved sufficiently to allow him to appear. Hearing dates had already been vacated once before because of his ill health.

The late Gopal Sri Ram was a controversial appointment. His reputation was mixed. Some thought he was too close to the ruling party, and yet others considered that in later years, he had become critical of the judiciary and what he described as political interference by the executive government.

In a reported speech given shortly after his retirement on 17 September 2010 at the National Conference on Integrity, Gopal Sri Ram said that the judiciary had failed in its duty to defend minority rights. He said that he thought because the judiciary had become so "executive-minded" that judges had become creatures of the government. He believed that such interference by the executive was clearly a breach of the doctrine of separation of powers, and the executive should never have usurped the power of the judiciary to convict and sentence. He was concerned that given the deteriorating condition of the judiciary since the 1988 crisis, when PM Mahathir sacked the Lord President (now called the Chief Justice) and other senior judges for not favouring the government, that Malaysia was failing as a nation.

When Sri Ram returned to private practice as a lawyer, his right to appear on behalf of a party at trial was challenged by his opponent, who claimed that his appearance before his former peers would undermine the administration of justice. The court ruled that the Legal Profession Act 1976 did not prevent a retired judge from appearing in court.[22]

---

22   See the decision in *Innovations Construction Sdn Bhd v MTM Millenium Holdings Sdn Bhd* (2013) Civil Appeal No: W-02 (NCC) (A)-248-01-2013.

Gopal Sri Ram conferring with lawyers in the defence team as Anwar looks on; Sri Ram with his assistant Lim Choon Kim.

That same complaint was raised against him when he appeared at the Federal Court appeal hearing for Anwar, but it really came to nothing, and Sri Ram abruptly dismissed any complaints. And so, he became lead counsel.

FEDERAL COURT APPEAL

There were multiple grounds of appeal dealt with by each member of the Defence team, which included Mohd Saiful's lack of credibility; multiple errors made by the trial judge and Court of Appeal; a conspiracy to fabricate evidence against Anwar; and the inherent unreliability of the DNA evidence and other related issues.

The Prosecution responded by relying on several grounds of appeal, which included Saiful being an honest and reliable witness; that evidence of other uncharged sexual acts was admissible as "relationship evidence" and provided context, and was relevant to assessing Saiful's credibility; and that expert witness the late Dr Brian McDonald, who was a molecular geneticist called by the Defence, was "not an expert to rely on", and had correctly been called an "arm-chair expert" by the Court of Appeal (curiously, there was no mention of Professor David Wells, a defence expert witness and also critical of the Prosecution's forensic evidence).

The Prosecution further asserted that the trial judge applied the wrong standard of proof at trial; there was no third male in the DNA sample extracted from Saiful's body; the evidence of the government chemists was to be preferred and that there was sufficient DNA in forensic samples to identify Anwar; the chain of evidence was intact with no proof of fabricated evidence; and there was no evidence of contamination of the forensic samples.

Anwar addressing supporters and the media immediately after the Federal Court hearing on 8 November 2014.

THE VERDICT

I remember the morning that the verdict of the Federal Court was delivered. It was Tuesday, 10 February 2015, and still dark when I left the hotel at 7.15 am. The journey to the Palace of Justice at Putrajaya would take about 40 minutes. The Federal Court was to announce its verdict at 9 am. I thought it prudent to leave early as large crowds were expected to be there in support of Anwar Ibrahim and security would be tight.

I had flown to Kuala Lumpur the afternoon before. I checked my email messages when I arrived at the hotel and was relieved to find that the Secretary-General of LAWASIA, Janet Neville, had sent me a copy of the Chief Justice's authority to attend the hearing as an international observer. Chief Justice Tun Arifin Zakaria had previously been most helpful in accommodating international observers at the proceedings. It was a relief, as his written authority would at least guarantee me entry to the courtroom. I hadn't come all this way to stand in the corridor.

As the taxi drove with the fast-moving traffic along the freeway towards Putrajaya, there was plenty of time to reflect on what I had observed in the last decade. I had been an international observer at Anwar's successful appeal against his first sodomy conviction at the Federal Court in 2004. Now, years later, I was returning to that same court to witness the conclusion of proceedings for a second charge of sodomy. It was hard to believe that it was happening all over again.

Nothing had really changed. Anwar was still fighting a criminal charge that threatened to return him to prison. If the Federal Court upheld the conviction, he would be removed from the political arena and, given his age, was most unlikely to make a political comeback. Yet, just less than two years earlier, he had come within a whisker of winning at the 2013 general election. The opposition coalition which he led won the popular vote, but the gerrymander of parliamentary seats denied it victory.

After his release from prison in 2004, Anwar brought three disparate groups into the opposition coalition and for the most part kept them together despite the occasional conflict. The opposition was now stronger. New leaders had emerged so there was hope for the future – where before there had been none.

The government, however, was now weaker. The conservative elements led by former Prime Minister Mahathir Mohamad had turned against the incumbent Prime Minister Najib Razak. The ruling party was severely shaken after having come so close to losing government, and fearing electoral defeat, it had abandoned any pretext of liberal reform. Over the previous 12 months, the government had resorted to using the repressive sedition law against its opponents to intimidate and silence opposition members of parliament, journalists and university students.

There had also been dissent. The conservative Malaysian Bar, representing some 15,500 lawyers throughout the peninsula, marched in protest against the sedition law and voiced its opposition to the selective prosecution of Anwar. Students defied the university administration and brought Anwar onto campus grounds to deliver a speech. Student activism was a new phenomenon in Malaysian politics, and it was moving to support Anwar. The mood of the country had changed and it wouldn't be the same again. Convicting and jailing Anwar wasn't going to stop the quest for change.

The sky began to lighten as we got closer to Putrajaya. Police helicopters could be seen heading for the area and we came up behind a police armoured personnel carrier that was slowly lumbering along with its own escort.

When we arrived at Putrajaya, the police had already sealed off a wide perimeter surrounding the court precinct. A large number of huge passenger buses were pulled up on the side of the road, disgorging Anwar supporters who were gathering to march to the court building. My taxi driver was familiar with the area and he took all sorts of detours to get me close to the building.

I collected an entry pass at a table at the front door and then walked to where Anwar's supporters were massing and waving flags and banners. They were all very much contained by metal barriers and a large police presence. Uniformed officers were spread out in lines along the barriers to prevent trouble. Not wanting to miss out on a seat, I walked back to the Palace of Justice and went through the massive domed entry hall up the stairs to the courtroom on the first floor. Outside the courtroom, there was a throng of media and supporters.

I entered the courtroom and saw familiar faces. Anwar's family were already seated in the reserved seats and waiting expectantly for the judges to arrive. The public gallery at the rear of the courtroom was full and included foreign and local media, international observers, embassy staff, special branch police officers and supporters. Anwar was walking around the courtroom shaking hands, joking and chatting with the crowd.

ANWAR: "I WILL NEVER SURRENDER"

At around 9.40 am, the judges entered the courtroom. The courtroom was called to order and the judges took their place on the bench while Anwar quickly went to his seat in the dock, which was located immediately in front of the public gallery.

Chief Justice Tun Arifin Zakaria, who led a five-member panel which included Court of Appeal president Tan Sri Mohd Raus Sharif and Federal Court judges Tan Sri Abdull Hamid Embong, Tan Sri Suriyadi Halim Omar and Datuk Ramly Ali, immediately began to read from a summary of the court's unanimous decision.

The judgement took two hours to read, but it was apparent early on what the outcome would be from the way it was reasoned. The conclusion was inescapable: the court intended to uphold Anwar's conviction. Anwar sensed that as well, and from time to time would turn around to look at his lawyers and supporters for confirmation. Finally, the Chief Justice concluded his remarks confirming Anwar's conviction, and it was all over.

Anwar's lead counsel, Gopal Sri Ram, then struggled to his feet – he suffered from an arthritic hip – and pivoting on a walking frame, asked the court to hear his client.

The Chief Justice agreed.

Anwar stood and, in a soft voice, started to read from prepared notes. But as he read his voice became louder and the pace quickened. His was not a statement of acceptance of guilt or remorse, but a condemnation of the verdict and the judges:

> I maintain my innocence of this foul charge.
>
> This incident never happened. This is complete fabrication coming from a political conspiracy to stop my political career. You have not given proper consideration to the case presented by my counsel from day one – that this incident never happened at all. I can go on and on, but I see from your statement today that it will be fruitless, it appears, as I have been condemned again, as I was in the Court of Appeal. Only here we went through a facade of an eight-day hearing!
>
> It is not a coincidence how the PM was able to release a full written statement on your decision barely minutes after you handed your judgement today – even before sentencing.
>
> In bowing to the dictates of the political masters, you have become partners in crime for the murder of judicial independence and integrity. You have sold your souls to the devil, bartering your conscience for material gain and comfort and security of office.
>
> You had the best opportunity to redeem yourselves – to right the wrongs of the past and put the judiciary on a clean slate and carve your names for posterity as true defenders of justice.

But, instead, you chose to remain on the dark side and drown your morals and your scruples in a sea of falsehood and subterfuge. Know you not that you are now wallowing in filth and foulness and the stench of your injustice will permeate through every nook and cranny of this so-called Palace of Justice and I do pity you all.

Yes, you have passed judgement on me – and I will, again for the third time, walk into prison, but rest assured my head will be held high. The light shines on me.

But the shame is on you for you will be judged by history as the great cowards of humanity. Sitting on that high horse of judicial power, you have stooped so low to become the underlings of the political masters.

Students of law and professors of jurisprudence will scrutinise your judgements, and as they dissect your reasoning and your decision, your credibility and integrity will be torn to tatters. And you will be exposed as the fraudsters who don the robe of judicial power only to pervert the course of justice.

Do not forget that, as all of us will have to, you too will have to answer to your Maker. You will have to answer why you turned your backs on the principles that you had so solemnly sworn to uphold.

People who come into your court have to bow their heads and address you as "My Lords" but don't you know that you too will have to answer to your Lord one day? By then, you will need more than bowing and prostration to justify why you wilfully transgressed Allah's command as ordained in Surah an-Nisaa, verse 58:

"Indeed, Allah commands you to render trusts to whom they are due and when you judge between people, judge with justice. How excellent is that which Allah instructs you. Indeed, Allah is ever Hearing and Seeing."

The judges moved uncomfortably in their seats and were clearly agitated at what Anwar was saying.

The Chief Justice turned to Gopal Sri Ram, who was seated in the front row of the tables reserved for lawyers, exclaiming that this was "not mitigation". Sri Ram replied that Anwar was simply exercising his right to speak. It was obvious the Chief Justice could tolerate it no longer and, after a brief discussion with his fellow judges, they left the courtroom together.

All the while, Anwar kept speaking.

There was no doubt that Anwar was determined to continue. He knew that he would get only one chance and he wasn't going to miss it. He kept on reading with his voice rising in defiance:

> Going to jail, I consider a sacrifice I make for the people of this country. I have fought most of my life on behalf of the people of this country. For the people I am willing to go to jail or face any other consequence.
>
> My struggle will continue, wherever I am sent and whatever is done to me.
>
> To my friends and fellow Malaysians, let me thank you from the bottom of my heart for all the support you have given me. And Allah is my witness. I pledge and I will not be silenced, I will fight on for freedom and justice and I WILL NEVER SURRENDER.

With the cry of "never surrender", Anwar's supporters chanted in unison the catchcry of his party: "*Reformasi, Reformasi*". It was chaotic in the courtroom as the police and court ushers attempted to restore order.

Anwar worked his mobile phone, giving interviews and telephoning key supporters.

The judges returned some 30 minutes later, and the hearing resumed. The Chief Justice announced that the court would not uphold the

Anwar giving his statement in court after the verdict was announced.

Supporters at the Jalan Duta Courts Complex, 28 March 2016. Anwar was due to appear
for a High Court hearing concerning the royal pardon that had been denied him.
"I will never surrender" was his concluding statement after the Appeals Court upheld
the sodomy conviction and sentenced him to five years in prison on 10 February 2015.

prosecution appeal for a higher sentence, and reaffirmed the five-year sentence of imprisonment imposed by the Court of Appeal.

With that, the court adjourned but it did not seem that anyone was in a hurry to leave. Anwar walked around thanking his legal team and supporters, and hugging his family who were clearly distressed. Forty minutes later (by then it was almost 1.40 pm), he was led out of the courtroom through a side door in the custody of several police officers.

Meanwhile, Anwar's supporters had moved to the rear of the building where Anwar would emerge, and gathered along the road leading away from the court exit to bid farewell to their leader. Regular police officers dressed in navy blue uniforms lined the roadway and kept the crowd under control.

By then, the police had already cleared a path to allow troops from the Federal Reserve Unit (FRU, a riot control force dealing with civil unrest) to leave the court building in their red armoured vehicles. But instead of doing so, the FRU decided it would confront the supporters with a phalanx-like formation of riot officers armed with shields and batons. Some FRU officers were armed with automatic firearms.

The officers marched down the road towards the crowd, banging their riot shields with their batons. High-pressure hoses were used to disperse the crowd, but only very briefly and probably as a warning more than anything else.

It was very dramatic, but all quite unnecessary as one senior regular police officer at the scene admitted to me. It provoked a few minor skirmishes and taunts from the crowd, but that was all. It soon became apparent that Anwar had been taken away from the court building by another exit and the crowds slowly drifted away.

Anwar comforts his wife after the verdict was announced.

Police and troops from the Federal Reserve Unit outside the courthouse.

FINAL COMMENTARY ON FEDERAL COURT'S VERDICT

The unanimous judgement of the Federal Court on 10 February 2015 dismissing Anwar's appeal and upholding the sentence of five years' imprisonment will no doubt be discussed and dissected in detail by others.

However, as I explained in *Anwar Returns*, I should at least provide some brief impression of the judgement. What I say about the judgement is by no means an exhaustive analysis of every point discussed by the court, but it focuses on the key issues.

Frankly, the judgement was unconvincing and lacked a detailed analysis of the facts on which it was based. It rested on two conclusions. Firstly, that Mohd Saiful was a credible witness and should be believed. Secondly, his allegation was corroborated by independent evidence and in particular the DNA material which proved he had been anally penetrated by Anwar.

In reaching these conclusions, the court rejected or ignored evidence that raised serious doubts about Saiful's credibility and the reliability of the forensic evidence upon which the Prosecution had relied.

Saiful's credibility was exposed by a number of factors, which included his affair with the young female prosecutor during the trial at the High Court; contradictory explanations given to Dr Osman when first examined by him; meeting with then Deputy Prime Minister Najib Razak at his house two days before meeting Anwar, with Najib's lawyer Mohd Shafee coincidentally in attendance; and meeting with senior assistant police commissioner Mohd Yusof at a hotel room that same night. The facts relating to the issue of political conspiracy are explored in more detail later.

However, the most potent evidence that the judges ignored was the forensic evidence. Putting aside other aspects of the appeal, it was the Prosecution's DNA evidence that was so comprehensively debunked by the Defence.

Obviously, if traces of Anwar's DNA were found in Mohd Saiful's rectum, and shown to be extracted from semen, that would be substantial evidence of penetration and ejaculation.

Ramkarpal Singh, in his submission on behalf of Anwar to the Federal Court, attacked the DNA evidence on several grounds, reiterating the defence experts' conclusions that were submitted at the Court of Appeal hearing in March 2014. He argued that:

- There was evidence of an unidentified third person in the high rectal swabs that had not been explained, which meant that Mohd Saiful had either been penetrated to ejaculation by another male or someone had contaminated the sample by handling it.
- The DNA analysis was inconsistent with the known history of the samples, meaning there was little, if any, evidence of degradation in circumstances where, contrary to specific instructions, the samples had not been properly preserved by DSP Pereira.
- The DNA allegedly taken from sperm cells had survived for more than 96 hours from the time of ejaculation to analysis, which was highly improbable according to scientific experience.
- The Differential Extraction Process (DEP), used to separate sperm cells from non-sperm cells, was incomplete, admitting the possibility that the DNA claimed to match Anwar's DNA didn't come from semen, but rather from non-sperm cells.

He made other criticisms of the extraction process and analysis conducted by the government scientist. He submitted that the government scientists had failed to meet "minimum international reporting thresholds", which meant in this case that they had been "selective" in identifying reportable findings. In fact, he said, Dr Seah Lay Hong's report did not accurately reflect the material she provided to support her analysis and she was at a loss to explain the inconsistencies.

The DNA evidence was the weakest part of the Prosecution's case, because both Defence expert witnesses concluded that while the DNA may have been Anwar's, in their opinion it could not have been obtained from samples taken from Saiful's rectum.

Ramkarpal was also highly critical of the way the Appeal Court judges dealt with the expert evidence called by the Defence at trial. The judges, he said, simply "brushed aside" the expert witnesses without properly analysing their testimony and dismissed them as "arm-chair experts".

Finally, Ramkarpal submitted that the evidence was such that the identity of "Male Y", which was alleged by the Prosecution to be Anwar, had not been proven beyond a reasonable doubt.

Any one of these factors would have been sufficient to raise a reasonable doubt, but in combination comprehensively undermined the Prosecution's case. Once the forensic evidence was gone, all that was left was Saiful's shaky and unconvincing testimony.

The court dismissed the testimony of defence experts Professor Wells and Dr McDonald on the basis that neither of them had performed any tests on the forensic samples nor had they undergone proficiency tests for some years.

This response was disingenuous because the defence experts were not laboratory technicians. They were called to testify because of their expertise and experience in the extraction and analysis of DNA, and to comment on the adequacy and reliability of the tests conducted by the government chemists.

Both experts raised serious issues that were not adequately addressed by either of the appeal courts. The Federal Court did not dismiss Professor Wells and Dr McDonald as "arm-chair experts" – which the Court of Appeal did – but the effect was the same. It was an unconvincing response to their expert testimony.

BREAK IN CHAIN OF CUSTODY OF SAMPLES

If one puts aside the testimony of the defence experts, there was an equally serious issue that couldn't be ignored. It related to what lawyers in criminal law call the "chain of custody" of exhibits.

The police handling of the samples taken by the medical examiners was sloppy and unprofessional. The containers with the swabs were kept by the investigating officer, DSP Jude Pereira, in a filing cabinet for 43 hours, contrary to the clear instruction of the doctors to freeze them.

Pereira admitted during the trial that by not placing the swabs in the police station freezer and taking a storage number, he had violated the Inspector-General's Standing Orders (IGSO), which were the same standing orders the court relied upon to justify his opening of the sample bag.

In reply to a question about that by Anwar's lawyer Sankara Nair at the trial, he said: "Yes, it [the samples] should be kept in a store. I broke the law, but it was my decision to do so."

But there was more.

Having admitted "breaking the law", he further admitted that before taking the samples to the government chemists, he had opened the sealed package containing the containers and relabelled them.

The trial judge was correct when he found that this was "not necessary since the receptacles were already packed and labelled by the experts who collected them. The whole purpose of packing and labelling and sealing by the experts who collected the specimen was to maintain the integrity of the samples and the chain of custody."

There was also an issue relating to Pereira's personal integrity that was relevant to assessing his conduct in handling the forensic samples. During the earlier appeal hearing, the Defence informed the Court of Appeal that an adverse finding had been made against him at a hearing before the Human Rights Commission of Malaysia (Suhakam) in 2009, which found him to be an untruthful witness. No mention was made of that fact in the Federal Court judgement.

Nevertheless, the Federal Court justified Pereira's conduct, saying he did no more than follow the IGSO to "put proper markings and labelling to exhibits for the purpose of identification in courts." It found that the way he opened the sample bag showed "transparency in his action" and the government chemist "did not detect any tampering of the seals of the exhibits."

My view is that by his actions, DSP Pereira compromised the integrity of the samples and risked contamination. He broke the chain of custody. His actions should have been sufficient to completely exclude the DNA evidence.

Whether the DNA evidence could be accepted would depend on the integrity of the forensic samples, the reliability of the extraction process and the interpretations of the results. The expert testimony of Professor Wells and Dr McDonald put all that evidence into contention and to my mind was sufficient to raise a reasonable doubt and it should have been excluded, as the trial judge had done.

EVIDENCE OF A POLITICAL CONSPIRACY

The Defence submitted at the appeal hearing that the prosecution of Anwar for the offence of sodomy was politically motivated. The Federal Court accepted that neither the trial judge nor the Court of Appeal explicitly considered what it called "the political conspiracy defence", and which it said, "if accepted, or believed, would have entitled Anwar to an acquittal."

However, the court said that the only evidence of a political conspiracy was that alleged in Anwar's unsworn dock statement, which was "no more than a mere denial."

As such, it did not amount to a credible defence and the court found that "the defence of political conspiracy remains a mere allegation unsubstantiated by any credible evidence."

Of course, it's true there was no direct evidence of a political conspiracy, but apart from Anwar's dock statement, the circumstantial evidence was strong and capable of suggesting collusion.

The judgement particularised meetings and communications between Mohd Saiful and "prominent persons, including adversaries of [Anwar]" before and after the alleged sexual assault.

These particulars came from Mohd Saiful's testimony at trial.

He testified that he met with then Deputy Prime Minister Najib Razak at his home on 24 June 2008, having been taken there by the DPM's special officer. Also present at the house was Mr Najib's personal lawyer, Shafee Abdullah (who was to later prosecute the appeals against Anwar), who told me during the court hearing that coincidentally, he had at the time been in the kitchen giving legal advice to the DPM's wife about another matter and had not spoken with Mohd Saiful.

Mohd Saiful admitted that he secretly met with Senior Assistant Police Commissioner Rodwan Mohd Yusof, that same evening, in a hotel room at Kuala Lumpur. He told the court that the next day, he contacted the Inspector-General of Police Musa Hassan, who was accused by Anwar of fabricating evidence against him when he led the police investigation in 1998. The fact that he was meeting with senior police officers before the alleged offence was committed was circumstantially strong evidence of collusion.

The sexual assault was alleged to have occurred on the afternoon of 26 June 2008. The day after, he met with a senior MP and officials of the ruling party. All of these meetings and conversations happened before his complaint to the police, which was not made until 28 June 2008.

Mr Najib initially denied meeting with Mohd Saiful, but he was later forced to admit that he had done so after a photograph emerged showing Mohd Saiful with one of his senior staff. He then attempted to pass it off as an inquiry about obtaining a scholarship, but finally three days later, on 3 July 2008, he conceded that Mohd Saiful did go to his house, at which time he revealed that he was being sodomised by Anwar.

I have no idea whether there was a political conspiracy or not. That is for others to decide. But the circumstances surrounding the alleged sexual assault were all highly suspicious. The meetings and communications with senior politicians and police before and after the alleged assault obviously had everything to do with Anwar.

There was also another curious aspect. Why did Mohd Saiful, after making his complaint to these people, go back to his employment with Anwar when there was every expectation he would be sexually assaulted again? He didn't need to return because he had already reported what was happening, to Najib and senior police officers. It just doesn't make sense.

Karpal Singh told me that these meetings were to ensure that there was sufficient evidence to convict Anwar. He said it was all contrived and arranged so that the false accusation would stand up under the scrutiny that would inevitably follow once Mohd Saiful made the police complaint.

However, suspicion is not enough. The true test of whether the offence occurred was whether the evidence was sufficient to prove the charge beyond a reasonable doubt. It is my firm view, for the reasons briefly explored in this book, that the state of the evidence was not sufficient to convict Anwar, and he should have been acquitted.

Anwar first stood trial over 25 years ago, in 1998. He was convicted and sent to prison for acts of sodomy and corruption. It wasn't until 2004 that the sodomy conviction was overturned on appeal, but by then he had spent six years in prison.

The conduct of these trials met with international condemnation of what many thought were substantial instances of procedural irregularities and judicial unfairness. There had also been allegations of corrupt conduct by the police and the Prosecution.

When I interviewed Anwar in 2013, I asked him whether he thought the judiciary had in any way changed for the better since his first series of trials in 1998. He acknowledged his acquittal by a judge of the High Court in January 2012, saying that was obviously a reflection of how some judges of that court were prepared to be independent, but he saw no real change at the time in political trials at higher levels.

He further explained: "In the lower court, judges ... a few of them ... tend to be fiercely independent, but the Court of Appeal and Federal Court seem to be more submissive because of the prospect of elevation and the position accorded to them and the guarantees of lucrative office after retirement." He didn't think that the judiciary – except in the lower courts – had shown much independence in recent times.

Asked if he thought the decisions made in cases affecting the government were predictable, he replied: "If you go to the higher court, then people can anticipate fairly well what the result will be and which is not necessarily based on the facts or the law."

It was clear to me in 2015 that politics had effectively destroyed the independence of the Malaysian judiciary and diminished the reputation of the prosecution service.

Things were to change in 2018, after Anwar's release from prison following an unconditional pardon from the Yang di-Pertuan Agong. His release happened immediately following the general election that year, which saw the defeat of the Barisan Nasional government.

CHAPTER 4

GE14: Victory at Last

In my book *Anwar Returns*, I covered the lead-up to GE14, which was conducted against the background of the 1MDB financial scandal. Dissatisfaction with the ruling coalition continued to gain momentum. Street protests were increasing, calling on Najib to resign. Mahathir even joined some of the street protests, addressing the crowds and wearing the distinctive "Bersih" yellow t-shirt.

Mahathir had never been satisfied with any leader who came after him, whether it was Abdullah Badawi or Najib Razak. He always thought that his way was the only way, and if they weren't doing what he wanted them to do, he publicly criticised them.

The ruling coalition was seen by many as corrupt and profligate. The Malaysian political cartoonist, Zulkiflee Anwar Haque (better known as "Zunar"), skilfully depicted both Najib and his wife, Rosmah, as being greedy and corrupt.

That image was fortified when police raided Najib's several properties on 17 May 2018. Police who raided the properties found them filled with millions of US dollars' worth of expensive handbags, jewellery, luxury watches and RM116 million in cash. The total value of the haul was around RM1.1 billion. Five police trucks were needed to cart away the seized items. The police commissioner told the media: "I think this is the biggest seizure in Malaysian history."[1]

---

1   *The Australian*, 28 June 2018

Apart from the 1MDB scandal, which had originally been exposed by the *Wall Street Journal*, Malaysians were suffering from an unpopular Goods and Services Tax (GST) that had been imposed on them in 2015.

The government had become increasingly authoritarian in its attempt to crush criticism and silence dissent. Najib had initially attempted to repeal some of the oppressive public order laws, but as the pressure on his government increased, conservative forces within his own coalition pushed him in the opposite direction. Najib, to a large extent, had been the architect of his own downfall. He had won the 2013 general election by trickery and corrupt practice, but this time it wasn't enough.

The opposition won the election because of an alliance between former foes Mahathir and Anwar. The history between then was ruthless and bitter. Nevertheless, they had managed to put aside their differences to join forces to depose the Najib government.

Many did not trust Mahathir, but by necessity Anwar was prepared to give "the old man" the chance to redeem himself. He publicly stated that it was Mahathir's commitment to reform that persuaded him that he could be trusted and relied upon. There just wasn't any other option with Anwar in prison at that time.

The government suffered a crushing election defeat. Despite every attempt to hijack the election, it failed dismally despite all the usual trickery and fraud. The defeated government was slow to concede the election, hoping it could salvage a win, but Mahathir was having none of that. He immediately claimed victory and called for the prime minister to be appointed at once, stressing that Najib's role as an interim government was "now over".

Mahathir was not sworn in immediately. He had to wait five hours while the King interviewed the leaders of the four parties in the coalition alliance. There was some suggestion that the King favoured appointing Wan Azizah as the prime minister, rather than Mahathir, who was not a favourite after having removed the legal immunity of royalty in 1993. In an interview on 27 January 2023, Anwar confirmed this was so.

Anyway, the alliance held firm and the parties stuck to the agreement that Mahathir would be prime minister if they won the election. Mahathir was sworn in as prime minister at 9 pm.

The understanding between the alliance parties was that if the alliance won the election, Mahathir would become prime minister for about two years, then hand over to Anwar. To be eligible to be a member of parliament, Anwar would need to be pardoned by the King, otherwise he would be precluded from running for office for five years after his release.

It was expected that Anwar's pardon and release from prison would take some time, but it did not take weeks as everyone expected, because the King had already made up his mind about what to do and agreed to an immediate pardon for Anwar.

THE MAHATHIR-ANWAR DEAL

The reality was that the arrangement with Mahathir was the only option available because Anwar was still in prison and did not have a parliamentary seat. His daughter, Nurul Izzah, flew to London to meet with Mahathir to seal the deal.

A royal pardon was part of the deal with Mahathir: the agreement was that if the opposition won the election, Mahathir would be nominated as prime minister and Wan Azizah would become deputy prime minister. Anwar would, on his release, "immediately hold a role within the federal government, and then be appointed as a candidate for the eighth prime minister."

The four partners to the Pakatan Harapan alliance agreed to the deal. They were Mahathir's Parti Pribumi Bersatu Malaysia, Anwar's Parti Keadilan Rakyat (PKR), the Chinese-centric Democratic Action Party and moderate Islamic party Parti Amanah Nasional. The

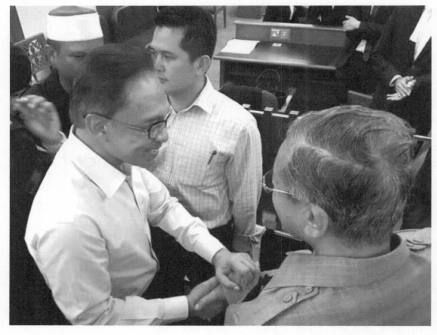

Anwar and Mahathir meet for the first time in 18 years, 5 September 2016.

agreement was in the form of a written undertaking which Mahathir signed, as did leaders of the other opposition parties. It was signed on 6 January 2018.

The document set out the policy ambitions of the coalition parties, which included such things as restoring the economy to ease the cost of living for the people; abolishing the GST; implementing comprehensive reform; a pledge for good governance and integrity; ridding the country of corruption; limiting the tenure of the prime minister to two elections; reviewing the national tax system; and ensuring the independence of legal and political institutions.

The agreement was careful to acknowledge the primacy of the Malays in respect to their language, religion and the "nobility of the rulers", which was expressed as the "special rights of Malays". However, it also acknowledged freedom of religion and the "legitimate rights of all races".

The political agreement was significant because it mapped out the power structure and, importantly, the transition from Mahathir to Anwar Ibrahim. The agreement was written in Malay, but this is the relevant English translation:

> Recognising Pakatan Harapan as a grand coalition of political parties that pairs two great statesmen, Tun Dr Mahathir Mohamad as the Chairman and Datuk Seri Anwar Ibrahim as the Chief of Staff to fulfil the legacy of the long-delayed mission, we are pleased and respectfully announce:

> 1. Yang Amat Berbahagia Tun Dr Mahathir as a candidate for Prime Minister and Datuk Seri Wan Azizah binti Datuk Dr Wan Ismail as a candidate for Deputy Prime Minister once Pakatan Harapan gets the people's mandate to form a federal government after the 14th General Election.

2. To strengthen the leadership of the Pakatan Harapan government and firm up the consensus among the political parties, the legal application to seek a royal pardon to release Datuk Seri Anwar Ibrahim will be expedited after Pakatan Harapan takes over the administration of the country so that Datuk Seri Anwar Ibrahim can immediately hold a role within the Federal Government, and then be appointed as a candidate for the 8th Prime Minister.

3. In preparation to overcome and win the PRU14 [elections], the Pakatan Harapan Parliamentary distribution of seats for Peninsular Malaysia, which involves 165 seats, is as follows:

   a. Parti Pribumi Bersatu Malaysia (PPBM)/Malaysian United Indigenous Party – 52 seats

   b. Parti Keadilan Rakyat (KEADILAN)/People's Justice Party – 51 seats

   c. Parti Tindakan Demokratik Malaysia (DAP)/ Democratic Action Party – 35 seats

   d. Parti Amanah Negara (AMANAH)/National Trust Party – 27 seats

With this, we reach a consensus that this agreement serves as a promise that binds our parties together.

The document was signed by all parties:

Tun Dr Mahathir Mohamad
Chairman [of the] Malaysian United Indigenous Party
Parti Pribumi Bersatu Malaysia (PPBM)

Datuk Seri Dr Wan Azizah Wan Ismail
President [of the] People's Justice Party
Parti Keadilan Rakyat (KEADILAN)

Tan Sri Muhyiddin Yassin
President [of the] Malaysian United Indigenous Party
Parti Pribumi Bersatu Malaysia (PPBM)

Tuan Tan Kok Wai
Chairman [of the] Democratic Action Party
Parti Tindakan Demokratik Malaysia (DAP)

Tuan Hj Mohamad Sabu
President [of the] National Trust Party
Parti Amanah Negara (AMANAH)

Dated: 6 January 2018
[Islamic date] 18 Rabiul Akhir 1439 H

MUAFAKAT PAKATAN HARAPAN

Rakyat Malaysia berhasrat menjadikan tanah air ini sebuah negara yang maju, stabil dan sejahtera. Mereka mengimpikan negara yang gemilang, utuh dan dihormati seantero dunia. Sejak Merdeka dan penubuhan Malaysia, pendiri bangsa telah mewariskan pedoman dan gagasan besarnya agar kita tidak tergelincir dari landasan tersebut.

Namun, mutakhir ini Malaysia berada dalam bahaya dan dilingkungi kebejatan tidak berkesudahan. Rasuah bermaharajalela, hutang negara menggunung, nilai ringgit susut dan hilang daya-saing, sedangkan rakyat terbeban dan menderita kerana harga barang serta kos perkhidmatan terus meningkat dalam keadaan pendapatan tidak mencukupi.

Justeru, menjadi keutamaan Pakatan Harapan menawarkan harapan baharu buat seluruh warganegara demi perjuangan membela rakyat dan membina semula Malaysia yang lebih baik.

MAKA, Pakatan Harapan bermuafakat dan bertekad untuk melaksanakan janji-janji berikut apabila Pakatan Harapan mendapat mandat rakyat untuk membentuk Kerajaan Persekutuan selepas Pilihanraya Umum ke-14:

1. Membentuk sebuah kabinet berwibawa; gandingan yang berpengalaman, berkelayakan dan berkemampuan;

2. Menjadikan Parlimen sebagai sebuah institusi yang kukuh dan bebas; dan dipimpin oleh Yang di-Pertua yang adil dan berwibawa.

3. Mengambil langkah-langkah segera memulihkan ekonomi negara dan meringankan beban kos sara hidup rakyat. Antaranya menghapuskan Cukai Barangan dan Perkhidmatan (GST), menstabilkan harga petrol dan memberikan fokus utama kepada usaha menambah pendapatan rakyat;

4. Melaksanakan reformasi menyeluruh demi mengembalikan maruah dan jatidiri negara dan Bangsa Malaysia, meliputi reformasi institusi, reformasi pendidikan, reformasi ekonomi dan reformasi sosial seperti yang terkandung dalam Manifesto Pakatan Harapan;

5. Menghadkan tempoh memegang jawatan Perdana Menteri kepada dua penggal pilihanraya untuk memugar dan menyihatkan amalan demokrasi terbaik serta mempertegas prinsip kebertanggungjawaban dalam urustadbir negara;

6. Memastikan ketua-ketua institusi penting negara termasuk Peguam Negara, Ketua Polis Negara, Panglima Angkatan Tentera, Ketua Pesuruhjaya Suruhanjaya Pencegahan Rasuah Malaysia, Pengerusi Suruhanjaya Pilihanraya Malaysia dan Ketua Audit Negara bebas daripada pengaruh penguasa politik. Mereka bertanggungjawab sepenuhnya kepada rakyat menerusi institusi parlimen, di mana mereka akan melalui proses pengesahan Jawatankuasa Pilihan Parlimen

(Parlimentary Select Committee) dan akhirnya dilantik oleh Yang Di-Pertuan Agong;

7. Membersihkan Malaysia dari najis rasuah dengan mendakwa pelaku rasuah di mahkamah, dan jika disabit bersalah maka akan dikenakan hukuman setimpal;

8. Memastikan institusi-institusi awam seperti FELDA, Tabung Haji, Kumpulan Wang Simpanan Pekerja dan Majlis Amanah Rakyat diurus secara cekap, telus dan beramanah;

9. Membela kebajikan rakyat terutamanya golongan miskin, ibu tunggal, orang berkelainan upaya dan kumpulan berpendapatan rendah;

10. Merapatkan jurang pembangunan antara bandar dan desa, serta antara wilayah dengan tumpuan khusus kepada hak rakyat Sabah dan Sarawak sejajar dengan semangat Perjanjian Malaysia 1963;

11. Mengkaji semula sistem percukaian negara untuk memastikan pembayar cukai, terutamanya golongan kelas menengah, tidak tertekan dengan bebanan cukai yang berganda;

12. Menghormati prinsip keluhuran perlembagaan dan kedaulatan undang-undang; dan

13. Menjunjung prinsip-prinsip utama Perlembagaan Persekutuan yang mengiktiraf kedudukan Islam sebagai Agama Persekutuan, hak setiap individu untuk mengamalkan ajaran agama masing-masing, kedudukan istimewa orang Melayu dan anak negeri Sabah dan Sarawak serta hak-hak yang sah untuk semua kaum, Bahasa Melayu sebagai Bahasa Kebangsaan dan kemuliaan institusi Raja-Raja Melayu.

MENGHARGAI bahawa Pakatan Harapan adalah sebuah gabungan besar (grand coalition) parti-parti politik yang menggandingkan dua tokoh negarawan ulung, iaitu Tun Dr Mahathir Mohamad sebagai Pengerusi dan Datuk Seri Anwar Ibrahim sebagai Ketua Umum dalam rangka menyempurnakan legasi misi tertangguh, maka Pakatan Harapan dengan penuh sukacita dan ta'zimnya mengumumkan:

1. Yang Amat Berbahagia Tun Dr Mahathir Mohamad sebagai calon Perdana Menteri dan Yang Berhormat Datuk Seri Dr Wan Azizah binti Datuk Dr Wan Ismail sebagai calon Timbalan Perdana Menteri apabila Pakatan Harapan mendapat mandat rakyat untuk membentuk Kerajaan Persekutuan selepas Pilihanraya Umum ke-14;

2. Untuk memperkukuh kepimpinan kerajaan Pakatan Harapan dan memperteguh muafakat antara parti-parti anggota, proses undang-undang untuk mendapatkan Pengampunan Diraja bagi membebaskan Datuk Seri Anwar Ibrahim akan dimulakan segera, selepas Pakatan Harapan mengambil alih pentadbiran negara, agar Datuk Seri Anwar

Ibrahim dapat segera berperanan dalam Kerajaan Persekutuan dan kemudiannya diangkat sebagai calon Perdana Menteri ke-8;

3. Sebagai persiapan Pakatan Harapan menghadapi dan memenangi PRU14, kami telah memutuskan pengagihan kerusi-kerusi kawasan Parlimen bagi Semenanjung iaitu yang melibatkan 165 kerusi, seperti berikut:
   a. Parti Pribumi Bersatu Malaysia (PPBM) – 52 kerusi
   b. Parti Keadilan Rakyat (KEADILAN) – 51 kerusi
   c. Parti Tindakan Demokratik Malaysia (DAP) – 35 kerusi
   d. Parti Amanah Negara (AMANAH) – 27 kerusi

MAKA dengan ini kami bersepakat dan bersetuju dengan muafakat bersama ini sebagai perjanjian yang mengikat parti-parti kami.

Tun Dr Mahathir Mohamad
Pengerusi Parti Pribumi Bersatu Malaysia

Datuk Seri Dr Wan Azizah Wan Ismail
Presiden Parti Keadilan Rakyat

Tan Sri Muhyiddin Yassin
Presiden Parti Pribumi Bersatu Malaysia

Tuan Tan Kok Wai
Pengerusi Parti Tindakan Demokratik Malaysia

Tuan Hj Mohamad Sabu
Presiden Parti Amanah Negara

Bertarikh: 6 Januari 2018
18 Rabiul Akhir 1439 H

As it can be seen, a royal pardon was part of the deal, as was the nomination of Mahathir as prime minister if the opposition won the election. It came to be accepted that he would remain as prime minister for no more than two years, and then there would be an orderly transition to Anwar. All the political parties making up Pakatan Harapan agreed to this deal.

Before GE14, Mahathir publicly stated that if Pakatan Harapan was elected, he would be prime minister for two years. He was reported as saying: "I can't stay for very long. At the most, I can last for two years."[2]

No specific time frame was mentioned in the Pakatan Harapan agreement, but Mahathir publicly acknowledged that the time frame for transition was two years, but as time went on, he began to suggest that two years was only a "suggestion" and that the period was not "set in stone". He told the media that "the priority is to return the nation's wealth and build our economy to become more sustainable."[3]

Mahathir was always quick to reiterate that Anwar would be his successor, but started to suggest there were reasons why it may take time, such as the necessary process of obtaining a royal pardon and finding a parliamentary seat. As we shall see later, the "old fox" was playing a game, which did not include handing over power to Anwar. All the while, he was scheming to exclude him from the ruling coalition.

At a hotel meeting of Malaysians residing in Brunei on 2 September 2018, he was reported as saying he would honour an agreement to step down after two years and hand over the leadership to Anwar. He was replying to a question from a guest who had voiced worry about history repeating itself on the choice of successor.[4]

On 10 December 2019, Mahathir announced that in spite of new sexual assault allegations against Anwar, he may hand over power after a

2   *The Straits Times*, 4 February 2018
3   *The Straits Times*, 9 June 2018
4   *The Straits Times*, 3 September 2028

summit of the Asia-Pacific Economic Cooperation (APEC) countries that Malaysia was to host in November 2020.[5]

However, four days later at a Doha Forum in Qatar, Mahathir, while acknowledging the agreement to step down and hand over the leadership to Anwar, suggested that he may have to stay in power after 2020 to fix major problems left by the previous government before resigning.[6]

It was clear that he was in no hurry to leave or had any intention of handing over power to Anwar. He would continue to play these games until the resignation crisis in February 2020.

MAHATHIR GETS DOWN TO BUSINESS

Mahathir wasted no time in appointing his ministers, which did not include Anwar. That was Anwar's choice. Mahathir asked him if he wanted a Cabinet post, but he declined, saying there was no need and, understandably, he needed to recover from his time in prison.

Mahathir did appoint ministers from other alliance parties, but it was obvious that he favoured and gave undue weight to his own party PPBM, which had secured the third-smallest members of parliament of the four parties in the alliance. The party with the most seats, PKR, wasn't getting its fair share of ministries, which was a legitimate criticism.

However, Anwar kept to the spirit of the alliance, calming down his party members, who had a genuine cause for grievance. In hindsight, it was obvious that Mahathir was securing his numbers in Cabinet.

Characteristically, Mahathir didn't consult widely, but pushed his own agenda. Many of the ministers were inexperienced and not up to challenging the "old fox" and did what Mahathir wanted of them. Mahathir promised reform, but as time went on, it became clear that reform was not part of his agenda.

---

5   *The Straits Times*, 14 December 2019
6   BenarNews, 13 February 2020

Mahathir was more interested in going after Najib Razak. He had vigorously campaigned against him in the run up to the election, alleging corruption and cronyism. He wasted no time in moving against Najib by preventing him from leaving the country and opening an inquiry into the 1MDB financial scandal. More of that later.

KING PARDONS ANWAR

Readers will recall that the understanding between the parties to the Pakatan Harapan alliance was that Mahathir would become prime minister for about two years if the alliance won the election and then he would hand over to Anwar. Before the transition to Anwar could take place, he still needed to be pardoned and released from prison.

At Mahathir's swearing in as prime minister on 10 May 2018, the King told Lim Guan Eng that he was prepared to pardon Anwar immediately, and that was exactly what he did.

At 11.30 am on 16 May 2018, Anwar was released from Cheras Rehabilitation Hospital, where he was being treated for a back condition. He walked with his wife and daughter, Nurul Izzah, along a corridor leading out of the hospital building and towards the waiting vehicle that would take him to the audience with His Majesty. His wife had her arm around his waist as a show of support.

When they reached the SUV, which was parked waiting for him, they were confronted with a throng of supporters and media. Anwar paused, standing on the vehicle's sill to speak, but the shouts of support were too great. So, with a wave and thumbs up, he slipped quickly into the rear seat and was whisked away to meet the King.

The King was waiting for him, so too was Mahathir. The audience took an hour, during which the King granted the royal pardon. The pardon was unconditional, without any admission of guilt, which meant his criminal record had been completely erased. Anwar was once again

Video grab of Anwar Ibrahim as he walks the corridors of
Cheras Rehabilitation Hospital towards his freedom, 16 May 2018.
His wife, Wan Azizah, holds him protectively as they are met
by their daughter, Nurul Izzah.

a free man and, together with his family, headed for his residence in Segambut Dalam.

Anwar later told me, when I interviewed him on 31 May 2018, that when he met with the King on 16 May 2018, His Majesty told him that he had read my book *Anwar Returns*, and was immediately convinced there had been a miscarriage of justice, which was why he had acted so quickly to pardon him.

PADANG TIMUR RALLY

That night, Anwar made a comeback speech at Padang Timur near Petaling Jaya. Despite torrential rain that afternoon, which turned the ground into a muddy bog, several thousand people turned up to hear him speak.

He told the crowd: "I give my support to Tun Dr Mahathir. We must give strong support to him and the Cabinet. I would not support him if I was not confident that he would bring change to the country."

"I have missed you all dearly," he told them as he ended his speech. "You cannot imagine what it is like to be alone in prison. I have the strength, but it was really difficult and tough. To me, all of you who are here, are so sweet and so loving."[7]

7   *New Straits Times*, 17 May 2018

CHAPTER 5

Going After Najib Razak:
Arrest, Trial and Conviction

In *Anwar Returns*, I explained that the state investment fund 1MDB was set up by Prime Minister Najib Razak in 2009. Malaysians were told that it would turn Kuala Lumpur into a financial hub and boost the economy through strategic investments. However, it started to attract negative scrutiny in early 2015 after it missed payments for some of the billions of dollars it owed to banks and bondholders.

Before GE14 in 2018, Prime Minister Najib, members of his family and several allies were coming under significant pressure, having been accused of embezzling huge sums of money from the state investment fund 1MDB.

At the core of the claims was the allegation that nearly US$700 million had been transferred to Najib's personal bank account. It was the *Wall Street Journal* that exposed the extent of the corrupt dealings, reporting that it had seen a paper trail that allegedly traced the transfer of money into his account.

Najib did many things to stall the issue. He replaced his deputy, Muhyiddin Yassin, who had criticised his handling of the allegations surrounding 1MDB. He also replaced the Attorney-General, Tan Sri Abdul Gani Patail, apparently on health grounds and who was leading the investigation into the financial scandal. He reshuffled his Cabinet to stack it with supporters, which temporarily eased the pressure and ordered that the investigation files of 1MDB be restricted from disclosure under the Official Secrets Act.

The opposition had campaigned relentlessly against Najib before the election, particularly his old boss Mahathir, who alleged corruption and cronyism, and there were mass demonstrations calling for his resignation.

Once elected in 2018, Mahathir was determined to go after Najib Razak. He wasted no time in moving against Najib by preventing him from leaving the country and opening an inquiry into the 1MDB financial scandal.

A report by the Auditor-General from 2015, which had been classified as "top secret" under the Official Secrets Act 1972, had been suppressed by Najib. On 15 May 2018, Mahathir ordered that it be declassified and released for publication.

It revealed that 1MDB was "insolvent" and unable to pay its current debts of about RM28 billion over the next five years. The newly appointed finance minister, Lim Guan Eng, commissioned a report by international accounting firm PricewaterhouseCoopers to evaluate the audit report and conduct its own evaluation to "determine the cost of the shenanigans to the taxpayers."[1]

On 11 May 2018, the police were informed that Najib and his wife were listed on a flight manifest of a private jet scheduled to leave from an airport near Kuala Lumpur for Jakarta at 10 am local time. This was two days after Mahathir was sworn in as prime minister.

Najib explained on Twitter that he was just taking a short break, saying: "After over four decades in politics and the recent election campaign, which was regrettably personal and perhaps the most intense in Malaysian history, I will take a short break to spend time with my family whom I have not seen enough of in recent years."[2]

---

1   Bloomberg, 23 May 2018
2   Reuters, 12 May 2018

However, Najib and his wife were prevented from leaving Malaysia. Upon the orders of Prime Minister Mahathir, the immigration department announced that both had "just been blacklisted from leaving the country."[3]

Najib tweeted, saying: "I have been informed that the Malaysian immigration department will not allow my family and me to go overseas. I respect the directive and will remain with my family in the country."[4]

It looks like he did not have much choice but to stay. It was reported that after details of his flight was disclosed, dozens of people went to the airport, including journalists. Riot police were apparently stationed outside the gate.

Elsewhere, I have described that on 16 May 2018, the police raided six properties linked to Najib and his wife, where huge amounts of local and foreign currency, and luxury goods, including designer handbags, jewellery and watches, worth approximately US$273 million were found. Police described it as the biggest seizure in Malaysian history.[5]

Najib almost immediately resigned as president of UMNO and chairman of the Barisan Nasional coalition. He took to Twitter to apologise for his "shortcomings and mistakes".[6]

However, the investigation was closing in on him and his wife.

On 3 July 2018, anti-corruption investigators arrested Najib Razak, charging him with offences of criminal breach of trust and corruption in connection with the investment fund scandal. He was held overnight in custody and released on bail the next day, calling his arrest "politically motivated and the result of political vengeance."[7]

On 4 July 2018, Najib was charged with three counts of money laundering, relating to having RM42 million from 1MDB deposited into his personal bank account. He had earlier also been charged with breach of trust and abuse of office.

3   *The Guardian*, 12 May 2018
4   Najib's Twitter Account, 7.30 am, 12 May 2018
5   The Star Online, 28 June 2018
6   Najib's Twitter Account, 7.30 am, 12 May 2018
7   *The New York Times*, 3 July 2018

Najib denied any wrongdoing, but on 28 July 2020, after trial, the former prime minister was sentenced to 12 years' imprisonment for one charge of abuse of power contrary to section 409 of the Penal Code, and ten years' imprisonment for each of six charges of money laundering and breach of trust. The sentences were ordered to be served concurrently (at the same time), but were suspended pending appeal.

The trial judge, Mohamad Nazlan Mohamad Ghazali, found that the Prosecution had proved the charges beyond a reasonable doubt. Najib told reporters outside the court: "I am surely not satisfied with the result. This definitely is not the end of the world, because there is a process of appeal, and we hope that we would be successful then."[8]

The charges related to the RM42 million transferred from the 1MDB fund to Najib's private accounts. His Defence team argued that he was led to believe the funds in his accounts were donated by a member of the Saudi royal family, rather than fraudulently taken from the state fund.

Following his trial, Najib appealed the conviction, which ultimately came before the Federal Court. During his appeal, Najib alleged that his right to a fair trial had been undermined. He sought to remove the Chief Justice, Maimun Tuan Mat, from the case, stating that her husband had previously criticised him on social media and that this could lead to bias.

In his affidavit read out in court by his lawyer, Najib said comments made by Maimun's husband were "highly disturbing" as they may have influenced her opinion of the case. The court's findings may be seen as "tainted with bias, and the public perception of the independence of the judiciary will be in doubt," Najib said in his application.

Najib, who replaced his legal team only weeks before his appeal began, also claimed his right to a fair trial was at risk because the court had refused his requests to postpone hearings to allow his new representatives time to prepare his case.

8   BBC News, 28 July 2020

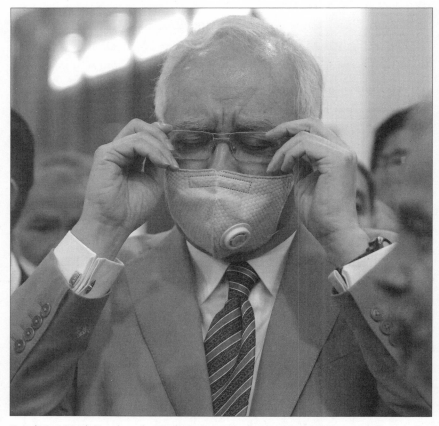

Datuk Seri Najib Razak at the High Court in Kuala Lumpur, 28 July 2020.

His application to disqualify the Chief Justice was rejected. The court also rejected his attempt to introduce new evidence that could have prompted a retrial on allegations of bias by the High Court judge who sentenced him in 2020.

On 23 August 2022, the Federal Court delivered its decision and upheld the conviction. The five-member panel of judges agreed unanimously that Najib's appeal was "devoid of any merits". Chief Justice Maimun Tuan Mat, who upheld the verdict, said the Defence was "so inherently inconsistent and incredible that it does not raise a reasonable doubt on the Prosecution case."

That wasn't the end of it. Najib sought a review of the decision to convict him of corruption. Again, he claimed that he had not received a fair hearing, alleging that the Chief Justice had a clear conflict of interest and that his new legal team had not been allowed enough time to prepare the case.

The Federal Court dismissed the application for review, exhausting the former prime minister's final avenue of appeal. "There has been no prejudice and no failure of justice," said Justice Vernon Ong in his judgement. The five-member panel voted to dismiss Najib's application 4–1. Justice Ong went on to say: "In the final analysis, and having regard to all circumstances, we are constrained to say that the applicant (Najib) was the author of his own misfortunes."[9]

But there had been more drama before the court's decision. In April 2022, the Malaysian Anti-Corruption Commission (MACC) revealed that it had launched an investigation into the conduct of former High Court judge Mohamad Nazlan Mohamad Ghazali, who had presided over Najib's corruption trial in the High Court which resulted in his conviction and sentence of 12 years' imprisonment. MACC chief commissioner Azam Baki said an investigation paper had been opened after official reports were lodged relating to allegations of unexplained monies in the judge's bank account.[10]

9   Associated Press, 31 March 2023
10 *The Straits Times*, 23 April 2022

Cartoon by Zunar

The author with cartoonist, Zunar, at the Georgetown
Literary Festival in 2015.

The investigation prompted a complaint by the Chief Justice Tun Tengku Maimun Tuan Mat that the investigation was done without following certain protocols, including failing to consult with her before commencing an investigation of any criminal complaint against a judge, and that the facts of the investigation could not be made public. She also questioned the timing of the investigation and press statement about it by the MACC, noting it came before Najib's final appeal before the Federal Court.[11]

On 19 June 2023, Prime Minister Anwar Ibrahim told Parliament that the MACC had completed its investigation and found no criminal wrongdoing by the judge. He said: "The MACC opened an investigation paper on Mohd Nazlan after receiving a report of his alleged involvement in a corruption case. The agency then carried out a detailed investigation and found no criminal wrongdoing was committed and this was agreed upon by the Attorney-General's Chambers."[12]

The Prime Minister also addressed the allegation of the judge's conflict of interest while presiding over Najib's trial. He said the issue was "conclusively decided" by the Federal Court, which found there was no basis to conclude that there was any conflict of interest affecting the trial.[13]

Najib Razak is the first former Malaysian prime minister to be convicted of a criminal offence and sentenced to a term of imprisonment.

On 1 September 2022, Najib's wife, Rosmah Mansor, was found guilty of three charges of corruption in soliciting a bribe for influencing the awarding of a contract for a school electricity project. She was sentenced to ten years' imprisonment and fined RM970 million. At the time of writing, she was on bail of RM2 million pending appeal. She was sentenced less than a week after her husband commenced serving

11 *The Edge Malaysia*, 24 February 2023
12 *The Star*, 19 June 2023
13 *The Star*, 20 June 2023

Malaysia's former Prime Minister Muhyiddin Yassin leaves the Kuala Lumpur
High Court after he was charged with corruption.

his 12-year sentence at Kajang Prison after losing his appeal against conviction in the Federal Court.

Najib is facing multiple graft trials in 2023, one of which alleged that he had tampered with an audit report on the 1MDB state fund to cover up wrongdoings in 2016 before it was presented to Parliament. He was acquitted of that charge on 3 March 2023, after High Court Judge Mohamed Zaini Mazlan found that the state prosecutors had failed to provide sufficient evidence to prove that Najib had abused his position as prime minister and finance minister to order changes to the audit report. He was acquitted without having to testify because, as the trial judge found, the Prosecution had not established a *prima facie* case.

His co-accused in the case, former 1MDB chief executive, Arul Kanda Kandasamy, was also acquitted of the charges.

This was the second 1MDB-linked trial faced by Najib. His acquittal did not affect the 12-year jail term he was earlier sentenced to for corruption charges involving RM42 million transferred into his personal account from former 1MDB subsidiary SRC International.

At the time of writing, a third trial involving RM2.28 billion in 1MDB monies is being heard in the High Court, while another criminal breach of trust charge involving RM6.6 billion has yet to go to trial.

There was another shock on 9 March 2023, when another former prime minister, 75-year-old Muhyiddin Yassin, was arrested on corruption and money-laundering charges brought by the MACC. The charges related to allegations that building contractors had deposited large sums of money into the accounts of his Bersatu political party in exchange for contracts awarded by his government during the COVID-19 pandemic. Two former party leaders were also arrested and charged with corruption.

Prosecutors accused Muhyiddin of sourcing US$51 million in bribes from companies which hoped to benefit from an emergency government spending programme called *Jana Wibawa*. They also alleged two instances of money laundering through the fund.

The MACC launched the probe in February 2023, freezing his party's bank accounts. It has been suggested that Bersatu was building a war chest to fund election campaigns.

Muhyiddin walked through a crowd of hundreds of supporters and political allies from his own party and PAS, as he attended at the MACC headquarters to be interviewed before being charged.

Muhyiddin denied any wrongdoing, pleading not guilty to the charges when the matters came before the courts, saying that allegations against him were politically motivated. He said: "I stress that I am not guilty, and I will face all charges against me in court ... This action is political persecution because they fear the strength of Perikatan Nasional," referring to his opposition alliance.[14]

Anwar, when accused of launching politically motivated investigations, replied: "If any investigations by the MACC are regarded as politically motivated, does it mean that no one can be investigated or arrested?"[15]

The MACC issued a press release, saying it had obtained permission from the Attorney-General to charge Muhyiddin, and further stating that "the decision made against any individual is based on evidence and facts resulting from investigation, and not at the insistence of any other party or factor."[16]

The Attorney-General's Chambers (AGC) denied the accusation of the existence of politically-motivated and selective prosecution against any individuals alleged to have conducted wrongdoings under any provisions of the law. "As long as there is strong evidence and facts that any individuals that have conducted wrongdoings under any provisions of the law, such individuals will be prosecuted based on the provision of the law without consideration into status and background," said the AGC.

14 Reuters, 9 March 2023
15 CNA, 9 March 2023
16 *The Edge Markets*, 10 March 2023

CHAPTER 6

The Unravelling of the
Pakatan Harapan Alliance

In *Anwar Returns*, which was released in 2018, I had asked what the future held for the new government. At the time of publication, the government was untested and there was no indication as to whether the alliance would function beyond the election.

The difficulty with political alliances is that there is always some uncertainty whether they will last. They come together for a specific purpose, usually to fight an election or to form a government, but they have to last much longer than that if they are to be effective.

I said at the time that in the euphoria of electoral victory, it was easy to overlook the difficult task ahead for a new government, but Anwar was aware of the risks and pressures on coalition governments.

Anwar, who was still in prison at the time, wrote a letter to his colleagues agreeing to forgive Mahathir, but at the same time cautioning them to be careful of him. Anwar refers to the letter in his interview with the author (see Chapter 1), which took place on 27 January 2023, extracts of which are reproduced later in this chapter.

On 4 March 2016, Malaysia's past and present opposition political leaders came together to sign a Citizens' Declaration (*Deklarasi Rakyat*) to demand Prime Minister Najib Razak's resignation from office, at a press conference chaired by Mahathir Mohamad.

The Declaration targeted the 1MDB financial scandal. The signatories included Mahathir, Anwar, Lim Kit Siang, Azmin Ali, Muhyiddin Yassin, Anthony Loke and 50 others. It also demanded the restoration of the integrity of public institutions, and the repeal of all laws inconsistent with freedoms enshrined in Malaysia's Constitution. Dr Mahathir told the media that the assembled leaders, despite their differences, shared "one goal". He went on to say, "We must rid ourselves of Najib as prime minister."

He was reported to be non-committal when asked whether the reforms pursued included the freeing of opposition leader Anwar Ibrahim, adding that the focus of the group was to remove Najib, which was an obvious side-step by Mahathir to avoid speaking about it. However, it was reported that former Bar Council President Ambiga Sreejevasan insisted that Anwar's release was paramount in pursuing reforms.[1]

In Anwar's letter to his colleagues referred to above, he told them that in joining with Mahathir, they should not deviate from the core of their beliefs and struggle for reforms. He referred to the Citizens' Declaration, emphasising that he was apprehensive about the strategy to join with Mahathir and others, and "being caught up in the games of the ruling elites and their cunning tricks to maintain outdated, obsolete systems."

He went on to say:

> I am more inclined not to be seen to be uniting with the Citizens' Declaration (*Deklarasi Rakyat*) group and to start to set a distance. Instead, we must advance our campaign for change, to defend the citizens oppressed by economic mismanagement, in keeping with the principles that we have carried with us all this while. The Citizens' Declaration (*Deklarasi Rakyat*), including Tun M, can be part of our struggle and participate, but our agenda must be for change, not to advance the Citizens' Declaration (*Deklarasi Rakyat*).

---

1   Channel NewsAsia, 4 March 2016

His letter shows his concerns about uniting with Mahathir and being swallowed up by those who had not been part of PKR's struggle, and becoming involved in nothing but power struggles to maintain the existing system.

The following reproduction is not the entirety of Anwar's letter, which is very long, but contains relevant extracts which have been translated from Malay into English.

Beware of Mahathir's Ploy

Greetings. Peace be upon you and God's mercy and blessings.

The issue I am addressing here must be analysed calmly. The essence of it does not deviate from the core of our struggle and is consistent with what was sketched out before. My concern is that you will only listen to me out of respect but not take it to heart.

Throughout our history of struggles, there have been challenging episodes which demanded deep thinking and counselling. Our latest issue is in relation to the Citizens' Declaration (*Deklarasi Rakyat*) that has dragged our leaders and their teams to be in cahoots with Tun Mahathir and Daim Zainuddin (former Minister of Finance in Mahathir government until 2001, when he retired).

We must steer clear of the danger of getting caught up in the games of the ruling elites and their cunning tricks to maintain outdated, obsolete systems. Even so, many of our friends believe the new strategy is powerful and the best way to go forward.

They say it can give us a new boost, as combining our strengths might topple Datuk Seri Najib as Prime Minister and bring about change. They are certain they can keep things in control and avoid any divergence. This clash of ideas among us is a tangle we must unravel, but it should not lead to personal conflicts or disputes.

My stand remains as when there was the initiative by the late Tengku Razaleigh Hamzah to collect signed statutory declarations [of retraction of support for Datuk Seri Najib]. The other leaders and I had then agreed with this, but I prayed for vigilance, and urged that we uphold our principles and the aims of our struggle.

Essentially, the Citizens' Declaration (*Deklarasi Rakyat*) remains as Tun Mahathir's document; flawed and not in line with our agenda for reform.

Its only focus is the removal of Datuk Seri Najib as Prime Minister due to the 1MDB scandal. This is obviously a departure from the basis of our struggle for freedom and justice, the rule of law, fighting the abuse of power and corruption, and justice for all.

The leaders seem satisfied with the assurance that all concerns will be addressed after Najib's dismissal. This is reminiscent of the conspiracy of the elite rulers that I alluded to previously. This is evidently in favour of, and beneficial to, the rich and powerful, while the masses will continue to be marginalised.

Do not be fooled into thinking that the statements condemning the extreme injustices during Tun Mahathir's reign will motivate him to make systemic changes. He is known for his indomitable spirit and tenacity, and is very focused on his agenda and not easily distracted. The lingering fear in all dictators and autocrats is the exposure or unravelling of the crimes committed and billions of dollars squandered [under his leadership].

My kind and generous disposition towards Tun Mahathir has never been reciprocated. Far from being remorseful, he displayed his despicable side by repeating the scurrilous personal attacks. That humiliation, sadly, did not elicit any response from my trusted colleagues and friends. I presume you are more concerned with defending the joint-collaboration and interests with Tun Mahathir.

Unfortunately, this will only embolden him to justify his past excesses. His style seems to have moved from repudiation to the denial and erasure of his past mistakes. (Wan) Azizah and I felt compelled to rebut that as a matter of principle and to defend our honour. Our statement was in reference to autocratic rule, and the need for vibrant discourse, unlike his dictatorial approach.

To us, the Declaration fails to address the concerns and welfare of the masses, particularly with regards to economic hardship and institutional reform. Those who are obsessed with the Declaration will definitely not accept criticism. I beg to differ and put forth an explanation.

Be wary of the Machiavellians who end up ceding power to their cronies.

We pride ourselves on being perceived as magnanimous and motivated purely by national interest. What is missing in our subconscious mind is the stark reality that the institutions of governance were destroyed, and what is disturbing is the absence of remorse and sincerity to support reform.

Both Tun Mahathir and Daim Zainuddin were the masterminds and aggressive exponents of crony capitalism. Through a flawed and corrupt process, which included contracts for the generation of electrical power awarded to the Independent Power Producers (IPP); privatisation of highway projects; monopolisation of necessities by cronies. It is clearly exploitative and burdensome to the citizens. It did not end with their rule and the ramifications [of those decisions] continue today.

You may have sensed my increasingly firm stance after my initial magnanimous and conciliatory approach. Like most of you, I was naïve and expected Tun Mahathir to be more open to change. The series of discussions between the leaders of Pakatan Harapan and NGO did not sway his obsessive personal vendetta against Najib but [it has not motivated him to correct] the corrupt and broken system.

It is absurd that after working with Pakatan Harapan, NGO and my trusted colleagues of the faith, he continues to insult and attack me. These outbursts and such behaviour prevent the possibility of meeting with my family members.

A friend once advised that I should not expect a 92-year-old man to change. This only strengthens my belief that the ruling elite will only try to resuscitate UMNO and ensure the resurrection of the old order:

> *The serpent that did sting ... now wears the crown.*
> – Shakespeare

Allow me to comment on your other questions. Apologies, but I can't help but feel shocked by the superficial, simplistic assertions that with Najib's removal, we will be able to usher change towards democratic accountability.

I have asserted to the contrary, and there is no evidence to suggest otherwise. I was also urged to show clarity and an unambiguous approach concerning the Declaration, and I have done precisely that.

But I resent the insensitivity in pressuring the President, and in particular Nurul Izzah, to pay respect to Tun Mahathir and attend his functions. You may want to appease him, but to demand such a sacrifice from my family, particularly after the recent taunts are so heartless!

My friend, the poet Tawfiq Ismail, once wrote in his youth a poem which I memorised and once recited in Bandung around 2005. It is titled *Memang Selalu Demikian, Hadi* (1966) ("*It's always like that, come on*"), during the era of the student movements against PKI and Sukarno. I seek permission that *Hadi* (come on) to be changed to *Saudaraku* (my brother) to read, "*Memang Selalu Demikian, Saudaraku*" ("*It's always like that, my brother*").

Setiap perjuangan selalu melahirkan
Sejumlah pengkhianat dan para penjilat
Jangan kau gusar, saudaraku.

Every struggle always births several traitors and sycophants
Don't you worry, my brother.

Setiap perjuangan selalu menghadapkan kita
Pada kaum yang bimbang menghadapi gelombang
Jangan kau kecewa, saudaraku.

Every struggle always confronts us
To the people who fear the waves
Don't be disappointed, my brother.

Setiap perjuangan yang akan menang
Selalu mendatangkan pahlawan jadi-jadian
Dan para jagoan kesiangan.
Memang demikianlah halnya, saudaraku.

Every struggle that will be won
Always has make-believe warriors
And the masters of leisure
That's the way it is, my brother.

And to Allah, I seek HIS blessings and good fortune.
May this battle be blessed. Amin.

Anwar Ibrahim
(This letter was circulated to the public on 16 May 2016.)

There are always destabilising factors in play in a coalition and whether they can be managed will determine whether it is successful or not. For example, there is the need to satisfy the demands of party supporters; to manage the ambitions of individuals as they jockey for power and influence in the alliance; and to agree on a legislative programme.

In the case of Pakatan Harapan, there was uncertainty as to how the government would perform. It was an inexperienced team. Other than Mahathir and Anwar, none of the appointed ministers had ever served in government, which was very different from being in the opposition. The new government had also inherited a terrible set of financial books, with the country's wealth having been sapped by the massive debts of the 1MDB financial scandal.

THE MAHATHIR EXPERIMENT: THE DOUBLE-CROSS

When last in power, Mahathir was an autocrat, but this time his own power base was overshadowed by PKR and DAP, both with superior numbers of seats, which was bound to cause tensions.

In hindsight, it was obvious that Mahathir never intended to hand over the position of prime minister to Anwar. He constantly delayed the transition, with many oblique reasons why it was not the right time. His main excuse was the need to tackle Malaysia's economic problems, suggesting he was the only one who could do it.

Bersatu supreme council member Wan Saiful Wan Jan wrote in a lengthy essay, published in 2020 by the ISEAS-Yusof Ishak Institute in Singapore, that behind closed doors, Mahathir was "both adamant and consistent that he did not want to see Anwar succeed him as prime minister despite his public statements (to the contrary)."[2]

Mahathir bullied inexperienced ministers into supporting his views, mostly because they were incapable of standing up to him. He was an

---

2   Wan Saiful Wan Jan, *Why Did Bersatu Leave Pakatan Harapan?* ISEAS-Yusof Ishak Institute, Trends in Southeast Asia, Issue 10 (ISEAS Publishing, 2020)

expert in dividing and exploiting tensions within the coalition to maintain his power. He made continual excuses for not introducing a reform agenda.

More importantly, he conspired with others in the alliance to prevent Anwar's succession to the office of prime minister. He did that by encouraging disloyalty from the more ambitious members in the ranks. He attempted to engineer the takeover by resigning as prime minister, and then persuading members of the alliance to back him as the prime minister, rather than Anwar.

DISUNITY IS DEATH

The spirit of hope that had welcomed the election of the Pakatan Harapan alliance collapsed because of the ambitions of Mahathir, and his incapacity to hand over power as he had agreed to do.

The old man's strategy to stay in power destroyed the Pakatan Harapan government and opened the way for the Perikatan Nasional alliance to seize power, not through an election by the people, but by the manoeuvring of ambitious men, who wanted only power.

CHAPTER 7

The Azmin Sex Tape: Signs of Disunity

In June 2019, a video emerged on WhatsApp, purporting to show senior Cabinet Minister Mohamed Azmin Ali – economic affairs minister and deputy leader of the People's Justice Party (PKR) – in a hotel bed in Sabah with another male. A few months later, several other video clips were widely shared with Malaysian journalists through WhatsApp and uploaded to YouTube.

Haziq Abdullah Abdul Aziz, a young political staffer in the PKR, came forward as one of the men in the video, while naming Azmin as the other man. He was expelled from the PKR on 3 July 2019, on grounds that he had broken the party's code of ethics.

In an interview with *The Sun Daily*, Haziq claimed that he and Azmin Ali first became intimate in 2016, but they had always kept their personal relationship separate from their professional duties. Haziq said he started providing Azmin with political support back in 2013, when he was still a student at Universiti Malaya. He claimed the private videos were leaked, and that he came forward for fear of his life. He claimed the videos were filmed without his knowledge.[1]

Azmin categorically denied the "vicious libel" against him, insisting that the videos were part of a plot to assassinate his character and destroy his political career.[2]

---

1   *The Sun Daily*, 20 June, 2019
2   Mothership, 4 July 2019

Anwar immediately responded, saying the video was "deplorable" and that "I thought what I experienced should be the last [time]". Weeks later, he changed tack slightly, suggesting that Malaysians wanted to know whether the video was genuine, and who had released it. He went further in a press conference on 17 July 2019, noting he had earlier argued Azmin should not resign while police investigated, but added, "If the investigations are conclusive, then he [Azmin] needs to resign."

Azmin responded angrily, saying: "Read my lips, tell him he must look in the mirror."[3]

Azmin's supporters pointed the finger at Anwar for what they claimed was a political conspiracy to damage him as a party rival to take over from Mahathir and because they had fallen out over an internal party election. Anwar denied any involvement.

Mahathir, for his part, said that no one needed to resign – yet – and that "you are not guilty until proven [to be]."[4]

Mahathir was happy to encourage the likelihood of a political conspiracy, saying Azmin Ali would not be so stupid that he would get himself recorded while in a sexual affair, and that the move may be a deliberate attempt to affect Azmin's political future.[5]

Of course, Mahathir had much to gain by encouraging conflict between rivals for the office of prime minister he then occupied. There were rumours that he favoured Azmin, but the more likely scenario was that he was quick to exploit the rivalry between Azmin and Anwar to maintain his own power, or to damage them both sufficiently to ensure that the path was open for his son, Mukhriz, to succeed him.

Haziq, together with five others, was arrested for the distribution of pornographic material. They were later released from custody. At the time, Haziq was also being investigated under section 377B of the Malaysian Penal Code for engaging in acts of sodomy.

---

3   Bernama, 17 July 2019
4   *Sydney Morning Herald*, 18 July 2019
5   Malaysia Today, 24 June 2019

However, the whole episode fizzled out. On 9 January 2020, Attorney-General Tommy Thomas announced there would be no charges relating to the distribution of the videos. He said the video footage had been sent to experts based in the US to determine if it was possible to positively identify the two men in the footage and that there would be no criminal charges because the footage was of a low-resolution and it was not possible to make an identification.

Azmin Ali welcomed the finding and thanked his wife and children for standing by him throughout the investigation. "As I have consistently maintained from the beginning, this video is nothing but a nefarious plot to destroy my political career ... I had no doubt that justice will be done."[6]

Azmin was one of three senior members of PKR who later defected to help form the Perikatan Nasional (PN) government after Mahathir's resignation. He was also an instigator of the Sheraton Move with Bersatu President Muhyiddin Yassin and PAS President Abdul Hadi Awang, who worked with UMNO leader Ismail Sabri Yaakob to fill the power vacuum created by Mahathir's resignation.

Azmin served as a minister in the PN government under PM Muhyiddin Yassin between March 2020 to August 2021. He lost his parliamentary seat in the 2022 general election to Selangor Menteri Besar Amirudin Shari, the PKR candidate who won the four-cornered contest with a whopping 12,729 vote majority over Azmin.

THE SHERATON MOVE (*LANGKAH SHERATON*)

Some months before February 2020, those opposed to Anwar were plotting and gathering their numbers. The known key conspirators were Muhyiddin Yassin and Azmin Ali.

Muhyiddin had been UMNO deputy president and deputy prime minister under PM Najib Razak. In June 2016, he was expelled from UMNO over his criticism of the government and the party over the handling of the 1MDB financial scandal. Together with Mahathir, he founded the political party Bersatu, which was pro-Malay and allowed membership only to *Bumiputeras*.

Apart from being a member of the alliance, Muhyiddin owed no loyalty to Anwar. He had, until recently, been a senior member of UMNO, and then president of Bersatu, while Mahathir was chairman. He was extremely pro-Malay and obviously distrustful of Anwar's links to the predominantly Chinese Democratic Action Party (DAP).

The other main conspirator was Azmin Ali. He had once been close to Anwar and was deputy president of Anwar's party PKR. He was Minister of Economic Affairs in Mahathir's Cabinet. It is hard to reason why he would betray Anwar, other than to satisfy his own ambitions.

There were some plausible possible reasons. He may have thought that Anwar supported his rival, Rafizi Ramli, for the deputy presidency of PKR, rather than him. There had been the release of some videos purportedly showing him and another male engaged in sex, which some alleged had been done by Anwar supporters to spoil his reputation and obviously his ambition to lead PKR and replace Anwar.

Pakatan Harapan (PH) communications director Fahmi Fadzil (now Minister of Communications and Digital) claims there was a "silent mastermind" behind the February 2020 "Sheraton Move". He nominated Saifuddin Abdullah, who was then PH chief secretary. Saifuddin had formerly been an UMNO member, but quit to join PKR after disagreements over the handling of the 1MDB financial scandal.

Fadzil claimed that when he spoke with some of Saifuddin's ex-staff members after the Sheraton Move, he discovered that he had been drawing up plans in a hotel with his team "war-gaming the Sheraton Move".[7]

According to media sources, Mahathir and other members of parliament were involved in discussions for a new coalition to avoid the changeover of leadership to Anwar. Apparently, Muhyiddin attempted to persuade Mahathir to join UMNO to form the government, but he

---

7   *The Straits Times*, 1 November 2022

refused to work with them, particularly Najib Razak, who was then on trial for corruption.[8]

On 23 February 2020, the supreme council meeting of Bersatu (PPBM) met at party HQ at Petaling Jaya. A one-minute audio recording, allegedly of the party's council meeting, revealed that Mahathir wanted to stay with PH because of his antipathy towards Najib, but Muhyiddin was already doing deals with UMNO, whose supreme council was also meeting separately that afternoon.[9]

That same day, Azmin's group of PKR conspirators met at the Sheraton Hotel, where Bersatu was holding its supreme council meeting. What resulted was a bold gambit to grab power by a hastily cobbled together PN coalition, which meant that PH lost its parliamentary majority.

Azmin then campaigned to support Mahathir to serve his full five-year term as prime minister, which involved efforts to collect statutory declarations signed by lawmakers as proof of their support for his premiership, which was intended to bring about a new political realignment.

Weeks before, Anwar had met with Mahathir to discuss the handover of power, following reports that several groups were seeking signatures calling for Mahathir to serve out his full five-year term as prime minister.

It was Anwar's stated belief that Mahathir would stand down as prime minister after the APEC meeting hosted by Malaysia in November 2020, but he told Mahathir the actual date would be finalised at the PH presidential meeting on 21 February 2020.

The meeting between Anwar and Mahathir took place two months after the latter's comments at the Doha Forum in Qatar, when he had suggested that he might stay in power after 2020 to fix the economy and other issues inherited from the previous government.

Anwar told the media that Mahathir assured him that he was not involved in the "signature campaign" for the prime minister to complete

8   Reuters, 6 March 2020
9   *The Straits Times*, 13 May 2020

his full term and that he "emphatically" told him that he would step down as promised.[10]

Anwar later confirmed that he knew about the conspiracy against him six months before the Sheraton Move, which resulted in the collapse of the PH government. He said he was informed about it by four UMNO MPs. He told a special Q & A session with the media in the Sembang Kencang programme on 28 September 2022 that when he heard about it, he spoke with Bersatu leader Muhyiddin Yassin, who told him that this was an opportunity to set up a Malay-Muslim government. Anwar said: "But I asked him how about the Chinese, Indians, Ibans and Kadazans?"

Anwar went on to say: "I know the Sheraton Move would not have happened if not for two or three culprits. When it happened, Mahathir thought they would all back him (as prime minister), but UMNO and PAS retracted their support."[11]

Mahathir was still officially prime minister. On 24 February 2021, after Bersatu leaders failed to persuade Mahathir to accept their bid for a Malay unity government with UMNO, he resigned as PM.

In the power vacuum created by Mahathir's resignation, the Yang di-Pertuan Agong appointed Mahathir as interim prime minister, but in a last grab for power, Mahathir sought to rally support for a non-partisan unity government including all parties, but it was unanimously rejected, with UMNO and PAS withdrawing support three days after endorsing the plan.

What happened? It is difficult to piece it all together, as conspiracies by their very nature are conducted in secret, but it is certain that Mahathir stirred up trouble to exclude Anwar. Muhyiddin, Azmin and others were intent on doing a deal with UMNO, to abandon PKR and DAP in the PH alliance.

Mahathir did not want individual UMNO chiefs for two reasons. Firstly, to embrace them now would do him considerable reputational

---

10 BenarNews, 13 February 2020
11 *The Straits Times*, 29 September 2022

damage. Secondly, it posed the challenge of admitting possible rival candidates for PM, which was not at all what Mahathir wanted.

Mahathir played his card by resigning as prime minister, expecting he would be reappointed, but without the prospect of having to make way for Anwar. It backfired, because the main conspirators joined with UMNO to form a new government. The "old fox" had outsmarted himself.

Part of his ploy was to call for a government of national unity. This was after the coalition imploded following his resignation. Of course, he put himself forward to lead the government.

Anwar's PKR and its two allied parties, DAP and Amanah, had on that day been supporting Mahathir to return and lead a revived PH coalition, but Mahathir's Bersatu party quit PH and attempted to form a government with UMNO.

Some members of the alliance, particularly the DAP, were prepared to do that, which was not only disloyal to Anwar, who had always backed them at considerable cost to himself with the Malays, but it also showed they were prepared to back expediency to continue as ministers, rather than face down Mahathir. It would have worked, except Anwar refused to allow PKR to back Mahathir.

On 24 February 2020, Mahathir announced his resignation as prime minister. The surprise announcement came amid speculation that he was trying to form a new coalition that would exclude Anwar as leader. After his resignation following Bersatu's decision in the meeting, Mahathir was promptly appointed interim prime minister by the Agong.

Barisan Nasional and PAS had initially supported Mahathir as PM, but withdrew their support after Mahathir mooted a unity government. They backed Muhyiddin to join the PN government.

Mahathir's ploy to exclude Anwar failed. He had expected the alliance members to rally around him to form a new government led by him. DAP and Bersatu backed Mahathir, but Anwar held firm. Without PKR support, there could not be a newly formed PH with Mahathir as leader.

The Mahathir-led government collapsed when Muhyiddin Yassin led a mass defection of MPs to form a new ruling coalition with the scandal-plagued UMNO.

There are varying accounts of what happened. One thing was certain, Mahathir did not want Anwar to be prime minister. He wanted Bersatu to break off from PH because he wanted an entirely pro-Malay party without DAP and PKR, but he did not want to join a handful of leaders from UMNO, who were facing charges in court or may be charged with criminal offences in future, which included Najib Razak, Ahmad Hamidi and some others. Mahathir was prepared to accept some MPs from UMNO, but not these men, because he knew it would adversely affect his credibility, having criticised them so vociferously in the GE14 campaign. He also disliked the DAP. Muhyiddin, encouraged by Azmin Ali, had no qualms about joining with UMNO.

PH declared that their prime ministerial candidate was Anwar, and that he had the governing majority.

The King was faced with two rival groups, each claiming to have the necessary elected members of parliament sufficient to form a government. In an unprecedented move, he chose to interview all 222 elected members to determine which candidate had the majority. The King, on 1 March 2021, one week after the Sheraton Move, opted to appoint Muhyiddin as the eighth prime minister of Malaysia.

Muhyiddin's government was to last for 17 months, after which it collapsed when UMNO withdrew support for him over his handling of the COVID-19 pandemic, the mismanagement of the severe economic impact and lack of political stability. Muhyiddin and his Cabinet submitted their resignation to the King on 16 August 2021.

Muhyiddin was replaced as prime minister by Ismail Sabri Yaakob, again without an electoral mandate, but his term was to end at the 2022 general election (GE15), which saw the appointment of Anwar Ibrahim as the tenth prime minister.

CHAPTER 8

Exclusive Interview with Dr Wan Azizah Wan Ismail
(6 April 2023)

Dr Wan Azizah Wan Ismail is the spouse of Anwar Ibrahim, but that is not her only credential. She is a qualified medical doctor, specialising in ophthalmology. After Anwar was jailed in 1999, she became the leader of the *Reformasi* movement.

She became party president of Parti Keadilan Nasional, which merged into Parti Keadilan Rakyat (PKR). She won the parliamentary seat for Permatang Pauh, formerly held by her husband, but resigned to allow him to win back the seat in a by-election in 2008.

She later won the by-election for Kajang, following Anwar's conviction and imprisonment in 2014. Following GE14, she became deputy prime minister in the government formed by the Pakatan Harapan alliance. She is also the mother of six children.

She stood by Anwar in his darkest moments. More than that, she made his causes her own, fighting against corruption and cronyism; when Anwar was in prison, holding the *Reformasi* movement together; keeping the family together when Anwar was either in prison or constantly travelling; being the first female deputy prime minister of Malaysia; and not least, undertaking the roles of wife and mother. All great achievements.

Q: Dato' Seri, thank you for agreeing to be interviewed for this book.

A: I'm happy to do so.

PROFESSIONAL LIFE

Q: Let's start at a time before you met Anwar. You studied medicine at the Royal College of Surgeons in Ireland, specialising in ophthalmology, and practising for 14 years before your husband was appointed Deputy PM. You were awarded a gold medal in obstetrics and gynaecology, so you were obviously a good student. Did you enjoy practising medicine?

A: Of course, I enjoyed it very much.

Q: Do you miss medicine, at least to some extent?

A: Yes, after I stopped practising, I missed it so much that I actually cried over it for about two weeks. After that, I resigned myself to the fact that I wasn't going to practise medicine anymore. So, I accepted the fact and moved on.

MARRIAGE TO ANWAR

Q: When did you marry Anwar?

A: 26 February 1980.

Q: How did you come to meet?

A: At the hospital, of course! We met at the hospital where I was working. I was a young houseman and he was looking for a wife. (laughs) Actually, at the end of my time at medical school, I had rejected a few proposals and by that time, I was "no longer in the common market".

Q: Did marriage change everything?

A: Well, not quite. I was on a scholarship, so I had to finish my bond to work in the government service for ten years. So, I continued to work until I finished my bond and when Anwar became Deputy Prime Minister. When that happened, I then resigned. Of course, that was the change.

Q: He was the firebrand student activist and later rising politician in UMNO. Were you involved in politics in those early years or content with medicine?

A: No, I was not involved. I was the wife of a man in politics, but I was not involved directly. I was his spouse and performed my duty as one.

Q: You have five children and now grandchildren?

A: Actually, I have five girls and a boy, so I have six children, and now I have 13 grandchildren. And if you count the others, there are 13 grandchildren. (She welcomed her 12th grandchild a week after this interview, and the 13th grandchild one month later.)

Q: Oops, sorry. Has your family been a great support to you, particularly during the difficult years when Anwar was in prison?

A: Yes, especially when he was in prison. My mother and father, my father especially was my rock and strength. He accompanied me everywhere during the *Reformasi* years. He was my support system, helping me and guiding me throughout that time.

Q: I recall watching your children grow up over the 20 years or so that I have been reporting on the several trials and appeals. They were often in court. They must have suffered greatly, seeing their father standing trial and being imprisoned?

A: Yes, the children suffered. They missed their dad and they were very young. They tried to be strong and not show it to me, as they knew I was also suffering. They never complained and were always very supportive of me. We are a close-knit family, and the children are very loving. It was difficult, yes. The youngest child was only six and Nurul Izzah was just starting in college. She dropped out for a year before finally being accepted again in one of the universities, which actually had to ask for permission to admit her.

Q: Anwar has told me he regrets missing his children growing up when he was in prison. Did that put an additional burden on you as their mother?

A: Being their mother has been a privilege, never a burden. I only regret not having as much time as I would have liked to be with them while they were growing up. I still feel a pang of guilt thinking about how I neglected them during the years when we were struggling to get justice for their father. But, they managed very well, *Alhamdulillah*.

Q: Did you have much support during those years?

A: I have many people to thank. My gratitude goes around to family, friends, family support system, my mum and dad, my mother-in-law, father-in-law and all the in-laws, and even friends that we did not actually know we had. Without us knowing, they helped out in many, many ways, and I am eternally grateful for that. The support was actually overwhelming, and that kept us going.

Q: Was it risky for some of them to help?

A: Many of them were sympathisers, even though the system was such that if you were a sympathiser, you may be penalised. Many had to keep their acts under wraps, even though they supported us. So many were supportive of us. The Reformasi Activist (Otai Reformasi) are some stalwarts who we call "Otai".

Q: Who were they?

A: They are the old *reformists,* who until today, though some have actually left us, left this world, never quit in their endeavours to see that one day, Anwar Ibrahim will triumph against all odds. Their efforts paid off.

POLITICAL INVOLVEMENT

Q: After Anwar was jailed in 1999, you became the leader of the fledgling *Reformasi* movement, holding the movement together, when Anwar was in prison. You became party president of Parti Keadilan Nasional (PKN), which merged into PKR. You served as party president, being the second female to lead a political party. PKN merged into the People's Justice Party in 2003.

You won the parliamentary seat for Permatang Pauh, formerly held by your husband, but resigned to allow him to win back the seat in a by-election in 2008. You later won the by-election for Kajang, following Anwar's conviction and imprisonment in 2014. When the Pakatan Harapan alliance won the general election in 2018, you became Deputy Prime Minister. Great achievements.

Did you enjoy politics, or was it something you felt you just had to do?

A: Many have called me the "reluctant politician". I never sought to be in politics. I entered it by necessity, to ensure justice prevailed. Now, I do enjoy serving the people of this country, being the voice of my constituents and bringing change for the better, wherever I can. I enjoy it not because of the position, but because of the chances and opportunities to help which comes with it.

Q: Was there more of an opportunity to do that when you became Deputy Prime Minister?

A: When I became the DPM and Minister of Women, Family and Community Development, my team and I tried our level best to improve things in the country, for families as well as the community. These positions provided me with the platform to bring change.

Q: Is there anything you are especially proud of during that time?

A: One of the things I am proud of was "i-Suri". I wanted people to appreciate housewives and realise the important work they do. My mum was not formally educated, but she was brilliant. She would always say that if she had been educated, she would have been the prime minister. "i-Suri" was designed to ensure housewives would have a safety net if anything happened to their spouses, via a minimum contribution from their husbands every month. I had a good team and everything we achieved was a result of teamwork.

Q: Was it difficult to juggle your political work with raising a family?

A: Well, you take everything as it comes. It was not easy to juggle both and to find the balance between being a mum with my family and a politician, especially spending enough time with the children when you must be away for politics. Juggling a career and family life was not easy for me, but it's the same for every career woman. With God's grace, it was done. *Alhamdulillah.*

Q: When I interviewed Anwar at the Prime Minister's Office on 23 January this year, he agreed that he couldn't have done it all without you. Did you feel that way about what happened?

A: He is my husband, so standing by him and ensuring justice prevailed was and is my duty. Even if something like this happened to someone else, I would like to see justice prevail. We wanted to change everything for the better and deal with many of the wrongdoings in the way the country was run. We all want good governance, but what does it mean? You have to spell it out, and you have to make it work. It cannot be mere rhetoric. You must work on it, and it has to work out for the good of everyone. That is what's important.

Q: My latest book is entitled *Anwar Triumphs*, but I really suspect it is a joint triumph for both of you. Batman and Robin, perhaps, fighting for justice and fairness. Anwar says he acknowledges the part you played in his political career, but was it just loyalty to him or something that you wanted to do, or both?

A: It was something that I had to do for the sake of justice. Wouldn't you? Wouldn't anyone? Of course, I'm married to him and I am loyal, but apart from that, it was something that I believed had to be done to uphold justice. Isn't that what Muslims are supposed to do? If you are a Muslim, you must uphold justice against all odds.

Q: Now that you look back, do you accept the pivotal role you have played in the political history of Malaysia?

A: I am grateful for the opportunity I had to play a role in the development of this nation. I hope I am remembered as someone who fought to uphold justice and who tried her best to make this country a better one for all Malaysians. In the future of our country, every single one of us counts. I think even someone who cleans the roads, or cleans the rubbish dumpster or whatever to make our country better makes a valuable contribution to this country. We all have our roles to play. I happened to play this role and I hope I will be remembered as someone who tried her best to do that.

Q: My sources tell me that when it came time to swear you and Mahathir into office as PM and Deputy, the Agong was reluctant to swear him in as PM, rather preferring you as the leader. Is that true?

A: The King wasn't reluctant in that sense. He asked me because at that time, all of us contested under the Keadilan's logo and I, being the president of Keadilan, would be offered the Prime Minister's post. So, he offered it to me. Of course, I said we already had a pledge and that we honour our pledges. If we won, Mahathir would become the PM and I would become the DPM.

Q: The cover on the new book shows a photograph of you and Anwar facing the media together after he was appointed PM. I thought it was appropriate to include you on the cover with him because it was also your victory, wasn't it?

A: I think it is the people's victory, not just for me and Anwar. Alright, we may be the faces of it, but the people behind us made it happen. We never forget that.

Q: Is there satisfaction in a personal sense?

A: I'm grateful to Allah that this thing happened, because as a Muslim, this is also *Qada'* and *Qadar*, the destiny. It is our destiny. I think victory is in the struggle. Because if you win, then okay, but if you don't, it is still okay. It is the struggle for justice, for good, for the rights of people, for the downtrodden, for the people who have been treated unjustly. That, I think, is victory itself. Win or lose is part of Allah's plan.

Q: Was it a proud moment of achievement after such a long struggle?

A: It was. I was also praying that such a responsibility can be carried properly, and we can translate it into something that will then mean a better Malaysia for all Malaysians.

Q: Dato' Seri, thank you for your time.

A: My pleasure.

CHAPTER 9

GE15: Hung Parliament

The 2022 general election, GE15, was held on Saturday, 19 November 2022. For the first time, those aged between 18 to 20 were eligible to vote, following a constitutional amendment to reduce the voting age from 21 to 18. The voting rolls were also expanded by 31 per cent or six million voters as all voters were automatically registered.

It soon became apparent that no single political party had a majority to claim government, which required securing 112 seats. It resulted in what is known as a "hung parliament", where no political party or pre-existing coalition has an absolute majority of parliamentary seats. It was the first time in Malaysia's history that this had happened.

Anwar's party, Pakatan Harapan (PH), won the most seats at 82. The next biggest group was 74 seats for Perikatan Nasional (PN), led by former prime minister Muhyiddin Yassin. Barisan Nasional (BN), which included UMNO, won 30 seats. BN was led by former prime minister Ismail Sabri Yaakob. Minor parties, including GPS, GRS, Warisan, PKDM and PBM, and two independent candidates, made up the rest of the parliamentary seats.

So, at the end of vote counting, PH came out ahead of its rivals, but Muhyiddin's PN made a strong showing, with the Malaysian Islamic Party (PAS) also polling well (PAS candidates won 49 of PN's 74 seats). BN did badly at the polls.

The King had suggested that the two rivals, Anwar and Muhyiddin, work together to form a "unity government". Muhyiddin refused to work with Anwar. BN refused to align with either, but later gave its support to Anwar, which delivered him sufficient votes to form a majority. After days of political deadlock, the King appointed Anwar Ibrahim as the tenth prime minister of Malaysia. He had managed to obtain the support of BN, and other minor parties and independents.

The first test for Anwar was a parliamentary vote of confidence. He convened parliament to prove his majority, after Muhyiddin cast doubt on his support. It was passed by a simple vote on the voices on 19 December 2022. "The ayes have it ... We have a sufficient majority, and it is two-thirds," said Communications and Digital Minister Fahmi Fadzil.[1]

The general election revealed a nation still largely divided by race. While a significant percentage of the Chinese and Indian communities voted for PH, the Malay vote was low. These communities were to a large extent motivated by their fear of an Islamist-centric government, which they thought would further marginalise them.

Prime Minister Anwar is more than aware of the loss of the Malay vote, but is determined to increase it, when formerly it was largely ignored. The rise of PAS was a surprise. It was very much cultivated by PN, when in power and at the election. Anwar discusses these factors in my interview with him on 27 January 2023 (see Chapter 1).

---

1   Al Jazeera, 19 December 2022

Anwar's Appointment as Prime Minister

CHOOSING CABINET MEMBERS

Anwar's first task as prime minister was to choose a Cabinet. The make-up of the Cabinet, which came more than a week after his appointment as prime minister, reflected the need to accommodate the diverse assortment of coalition partners.

The Cabinet members totalled 28, including 22 ministers, two deputy ministers and four portfolios in the Prime Minister's Office (PMO). The majority of Cabinet ministers – 15 of the 28 – came from Anwar's Pakatan Harapan coalition; six came from Barisan Nasional (BN), five from the Sarawak-based Gabungan Parti Sarawak (GPS) coalition, and single posts to Gabungan Rakyat Sabah (GRS), a coalition based in Sabah, and the independent MP Mohamad Naim Mokhtar. As reported in the press:[1]

> "This cabinet is a cabinet of a unity government," Anwar told a news conference. "We have set several basic principles: good governance, spurring the economy, and reducing the people's burden in terms of living costs."

"The most obvious sign of political accommodation," the article went on to state, was the appointment of BN president Ahmad Zahid Hamidi as deputy prime minister, who was, at the time of writing, facing 47 charges of bribery, money laundering and criminal breach of trust. This was a most sensitive but necessary appointment, to hold the alliance together. Anwar faced criticism for the appointment, given his principled "pledge to fight corruption and cut back on wasteful government expenditures."

On Friday, 10 February 2023, Anwar was interviewed by Bloomberg's Haslinda Amin for the programme "A conversation with Anwar Ibrahim", during which he was questioned about the conflict between his values and anti-corruption policies and his association with UMNO, led by deputy prime minister Ahmad Zahid, who had been charged with over 40 acts of corruption.

Anwar replied:

> (Hamidi) has been investigated and charged and undergoing trial and the courts should decide (the allegations) independently. I've made it very clear that the courts are independent. I don't think I should pre-judge the case. He should be given the chance, the fairness to be adjudicated by an independent impartial court.

He went on to say:

> You have to form a viable, strong government. As long as the (anti-corruption) policy is accepted and there are no more excesses, then fine. I should be given a chance. Which party do I choose, Party A, Party B ... they are the same when it comes down to poor governance and systemic corruption.

IMMEDIATE PROBLEMS FOR GOVERNMENT

The most immediate problem for the new government was the economy. Anwar had inherited an economy that had been financially drained by the corruption excesses of the 1MDB scandal.

There was also a significant cost of living issue to deal with and as Anwar was to discover, much to his surprise, that corruption was even more prevalent than he had imagined. See Chapter 1 for his comments in our interview of 27 January 2023.

Anwar announced that the main driver of restoring the economy would be based on four main strategies: rebuilding the economy, eradicating poverty, reforming democratic and legal institutions, as well as establishing a trustworthy administration.[2]

Anwar's concern for the eradication of poverty was not a surprise. It is something he has spoken about many times before. In our interview of 31 May 2018, recorded in my last book *Anwar Returns*, Anwar explained that his vision for Malaysia was for a "peaceful, multi-racial, democratic and just economy." He said, "I have strong views about inequality and the fact that economic experts talk about promoting growth, but very little about abject poverty and inequality."[3]

Anwar's early international visits gave some indication of his priorities, one of which was international trade. Of course, international trade is critical for the success of any economy, and it is always on top of the list when foreign visits are made by heads of state. When trade is the objective, foreign leaders often travel with a group of high-profile business leaders to sign trade agreements or memoranda of understanding (MOU) with the other country.

FOREIGN POLICY INITIATIVES

At the time of writing, Anwar had visited Malaysia's immediate neighbours, including Indonesia, the Philippines, Cambodia and China. He has also visited Saudi Arabia and Turkey, to consolidate the traditional links with Muslim nations.

---

2   *The Edge Markets*, 19 January 2023
3   *Anwar Returns: The Final Twist* (Marshall Cavendish Editions, 2018), p 59

His first overseas visit after being elected in November 2022 was to Indonesia on 9 January 2023 to meet President Joko Widodo. One priority was to discuss regional security, particularly the situation in Myanmar. The other priority was trade and foreign investment.

Anwar and Jokowi witnessed the handover of letters of intent signed by ten Malaysian companies to Bambang Susantono, who heads Indonesia's New Capital Authority. The letters expressed the interest of those companies in participating in the development of Nusantara, Indonesia's envisioned new capital on Borneo Island. Among the signatories were Malaysian companies involved in the electronics, health, waste management, construction and property sectors.

Anwar's next overseas visit was to neighbouring Singapore on 30 January 2023, where he signed bilateral agreements relating to the digital economy, cyber security and cooperation on the green economy. Critically, he signed deals for the supply of power to Singapore, and secured US$3 billion in direct investment in Malaysia. These deals were initiated by the previous Malaysian government, but represented a significant step forward in bilateral relations.

When Mahathir was prime minister in 2018–2020, relations with Singapore had soured. He tended to hark back to his previous views during his first tenure as prime minister, which led to a tenser relationship with Singapore, a more heightened focus on the Israel-Palestine issue, and distant ties with the US. It brought back tension over such longstanding issues as the water agreement and the "crooked" bridge proposal to link the two countries, which was one of Mahathir's pet projects that was abandoned by his successor, prime minister Abdullah Badawi.

The constant changing of leaders, coupled with the COVID-19 pandemic, not only affected Malaysia's economy greatly but also slowed down the pace of progress on several bilateral issues with neighbouring Singapore.

Anwar's visit to Singapore seems to have acted as a reset of relations between neighbours. The bilateral agreements signed by the parties were significant, but there was also a relaxation of the border restrictions imposed during the pandemic lockdown, an agreement to supply water and renewable energy to Singapore, and reinforcement of the support for the RTS link from Johor Bahru to Singapore, due to be completed in 2026. However, there was no indication whether there was any discussion about the revival of the KL-Singapore High Speed Rail (HSR) project, which was terminated in 2021 after both sides failed to reach agreement.

The sovereignty over several islands known as Pedra Branca, located at the eastern entrance to the Singapore Strait, is still a raw issue between Singapore and Malaysia. The dispute began in 1979 when Malaysia claimed sovereignty over Pedra Branca on a published map. The case was brought to the International Court of Justice (ICJ) in 2003 and the ICJ held that Pedra Branca belonged to Singapore. The previous BN government attempted to seek a revision of the ICJ judgement in 2017 upon what it claimed was the discovery of new facts, but the Pakatan Harapan government decided to abandon the proceedings when the hearing was set in July 2018.

Anwar's next focus was on China, to secure more investment in Malaysia. During his visit on 2 April 2023, he met with Chinese leader President Xi Jinping, and signed 19 agreements to boost investments in green technology, digital economy and modern agriculture.

China has been Malaysia's largest trading partner for 14 consecutive years, with bilateral trade reaching US$203.6 billion in 2022, but Malaysia also maintains close economic and security ties with the US, with bilateral trade reaching US$72.9 billion in 2022. So, it is a bit of a balancing act.

Economic sanctions imposed by the US and aimed at impacting on China's tech sector, particularly computer chips, which are crucial components of everyday electronics, are problematic when Malaysia is the world's sixth-largest exporter of semi-conductors.

Mindful of Malaysia's ailing economy, Anwar was keen to promote trade and investment cooperation with China. However, he has in the past spoken out over China's treatment of the Uyghur people. So, it is once again a balancing act between his advocacy of human rights and the practical necessity of restoring and advancing economic ties.

All political parties have enjoyed friendly relations with China, although the religious nationalism of the Malaysian Islamic Party (PAS) has the potential to damage Sino-Malaysian relations.

During Najib Razak's administration, Malay-centric Bersatu (PPBM) and other nationalist factions often criticised him for allowing the Chinese to make what they regarded as substantial profits. They were concerned that investment from China, and the Belt and Road Initiative (BRI), could weaken the political power of the Malays, which they have always zealously guarded. They also thought that investment from China had the potential to strengthen the status of the Chinese community in Malaysia, which they have always treated with suspicion.

Anti-Chinese sentiment was effectively stoked by Mahathir and his successors for political advantage. These sentiments influenced China to suspend three major Chinese-funded projects, including the construction of the East Coast Rail Link (ECRL).

Anwar's visit to China was an attempt to try and improve relations between the two nations and, critically for Malaysia's economy, to attract investment and trade. The trip was a major success for Anwar, securing RM170 billion worth of investment commitments from China, which would undoubtedly stimulate the Malaysian economy.

There is no doubt that Malaysia, as with all nations in the region, is faced with significant challenges in managing Malaysia's foreign policy amid intense China-US rivalry in the Asia Pacific region.

Anwar has always had friendly relations with the US. In our interview of 27 January 2023, he spoke of the warm note of congratulations he received from President Biden, after his appointment as prime minister of

Malaysia. He also spoke of Biden's support for him over the years, when then Senator Biden was Chair of the Senate Foreign Relations Committee. As Anwar said in the interview, he would be criticised for whichever country he engaged with, but his relationship with the US raises some complexities.

One of those factors will be the difficulty in maintaining the balancing act of not taking sides between the US and China, as the US attempts to persuade countries in the Asia Pacific region to curb China's increasing influence.

One commentator suggests that "warm China-Malaysia relations, thriving economic cooperation in particular, could be witnessed during the Anwar era, but the anti-Chinese sentiment led by the Malay nationalists and U.S. pressure are the main challenges."[4]

Relations with Israel have always been difficult. Mahathir and his immediate successors were openly hostile to Israel, condemning Zionism and openly backing the Palestinians. It reflected a general anti-Israeli sentiment amongst Malaysians, which was probably based on their support for the Palestinian struggle.

Anwar was widely criticised for his statement to the *Wall Street Journal* in 2012 that he would "support all efforts to protect the security of the state of Israel". That issue came up as recently as in the general election of 2022. Anwar's rival for the seat of Tambun challenged him to state that his party PKR was not infiltrated by Israeli agents. It followed the arrest of a group of Malaysians alleged to have abducted a Palestinian computer programmer wanted by Israel. After they were charged with kidnapping, one of them was seen on social media in a photograph taken some years before waving a PKR flag. PKR denied he was a party member.

There is an expectation that Anwar will take a softer line, and will not adopt Mahathir's antipathy towards Israel, while at the same time supporting the Palestinians, which he has done.

---

4   *The Diplomat*, 29 March 2023

Anwar has always had close links with Turkish President Recep Tayyip Erdogan, which has brought criticism because of Erdogan's poor human rights record. Nevertheless, Erdogan provided shelter when Anwar was being pursued by the Malaysian authorities. Anwar had spinal and back surgery and recuperated in Turkey in 2018. Their families are close, so it is really a personal relationship, and the support is reciprocated. Erdogan was one of the first foreign leaders to call to congratulate Anwar on his attaining office.

Anwar has long been a supporter of India, including cultivating a close relationship with Indian Prime Minister Narendra Modi while he was leader of the opposition. He realises there are economic and political opportunities arising from a better relationship.

The relationship with Australia has always been solid. Anwar was disappointed that the Australian government was not as strong as other countries in supporting him when he was facing prosecution in the courts. At his many hearings, countries such as the US, Canada and the UK sent senior diplomats to observe, while Australia often sent junior consular officials.

Anwar was at the time understandably disappointed with Australia's lukewarm support during his court battles. I explained to him that the Australian government faced the dilemma of whether to maintain significant trade links with Malaysia or to publicly back him, which meant being critical of the BN government and jeopardising trade between the two countries.

The approach taken meant that their support was discreet, when it should have been more robust. Australia has a close and lasting relationship with Malaysia, and as a friend it should have explained its position and been more publicly supportive of him.

It must be admitted that over the years, the Australian government has put trade before human rights. That relationship has largely been repaired, and Anwar told me in our interview of 27 January 2023 that he was delighted to receive a warm congratulatory call from Australia's Prime Minister Anthony Albanese.

COHERENT FOREIGN POLICY?

It is still too early to observe a coherent foreign policy, but Anwar has acted immediately to visit his regional neighbours and, importantly, China and Singapore. At this stage, the impetus seems to be economic, but it gets more difficult when it comes to human rights issues, which he has long advocated, and dealing with the rivalry between China and the US.

CHAPTER 11

Future Prospects of Pakatan Harapan Coalition Government

In *Anwar Returns*, I discussed the concept of coalitions, and the tensions that inevitably arise when disparate groups are brought together. Anwar had discussed this in our interview on 31 May 2018, reflecting on how coalitions do not last indefinitely. Speaking of the Pakatan Harapan (PH) alliance in 2018, he said:[1]

> Well, it will be a major challenge. It won't be easy, Mark. You know coalitions in a post-evolutionary phase have never been that successful. Of course, this is something known to the coalition partners. Throughout history, coalitions cannot be sustained, but then if we realise that is the verdict of history, then we have to do more to overcome that.

Inevitably, former prime minister Dr Mahathir had advice to offer, describing the unity government as "a coalition of incompatibles". He said: "They don't have the same objective or the same philosophy and yet they found a need to work together, so they overlooked all their past statements, past promises, in order to form this coalition."[2]

---

1   *Anwar Returns: The Final Twist* (Marshall Cavendish Editions, 2018), p 51
2   CNA, 4 February 2023

Of course, to hold the alliance together, Anwar made compromises over key roles, but that is how coalitions work. Not everyone will be happy, but to make it worth their while, there has to be something for everyone. Being the autocrat, Mahathir could not conceive of compromising one's interests for the general good. It was that attitude that brought down the PH alliance in 2020.

The Democratic Action Party (DAP) ended up with only four ministers, even though it had 40 members of parliament. DAP Secretary-General Anthony Loke acknowledged there was "some unhappiness" within his party, but that he thought the "sacrifice" was for the good of the country, saying: "[T]he alternative would be a government led by PAS. So, I think the Chinese community and, by and large, the non-Malays including the Indian community supported our decision to be part of the government even with the lesser representation in the Cabinet."[3]

Some pundits have observed that the future of the government may well depend on how it deals with the economy and cost of living. Anwar has acknowledged the importance of these issues, appointing experienced politicians to handle the key economic ministries, namely Parti Keadilan Rakyat (PKR) deputy president Rafizi Ramli as economic affairs minister and Tengku Zafrul Abdul Aziz, the former finance minister, to lead the international trade and industry portfolio. Anwar took on the finance portfolio, a role which he held in the 1990s.

One major challenge for Anwar is how to deal with the call for Najib Razak to be pardoned for his crimes. The deputy prime minister and United Malays National Organisation (UMNO) president Ahmad Zahid Hamidi at a recent party general assembly described the charges against Najib as "political and selective prosecution".[4]

Najib applied for a royal pardon less than two weeks after he was sent to jail for 12 years for corruption in September 2022. After his application to

---

3   CNA, 4 February 2023
4   MalaysiaNow, 18 April 2023

review his conviction was rejected by the Federal Court, the call for a royal pardon became louder, as he had exhausted all of his legal avenues.

On 7 April 2023, UMNO said it would appeal to the King to consider pardoning Najib, but the *de facto* minister of law, Datuk Seri Azalina Othman Said, has said that the Prisons Regulations provided that only a prisoner or his or her immediate family members, namely a spouse or children, can do so.[5] This means that neither a political party nor the prisoner's lawyer can petition for a royal pardon on his or her behalf.

The risk for Anwar is that if he fails to secure a pardon for Najib, UMNO may withdraw its support for the PH alliance, and the government would fall. It should not be forgotten that he came to power on the back of support from Barisan Nasional (BN), and its lynchpin party UMNO.

This is not just a case of handing out government positions or positions at government-linked companies or missions which carries little risk other than a general criticism over the waste of funds, favouritism or questionable credentials. Rather, it relates to criminal charges involving matters of integrity and corruption. The 2022 general election was essentially fought on these issues. Anwar Ibrahim has built his reputation on fighting cronyism and corruption. His recent pledges to fight both is a restatement of his long-held principles and his ambition to fight crime.

Anwar has no power to pardon Najib, or anyone, in a personal capacity. However, he is a member of the Pardons Board panel that makes recommendations to the Yang di-Pertuan Agong for a royal pardon. He claims there is no conflict of interest.

The risks are real. He and other members of the government say that it is solely the King's prerogative to pardon convicted offenders, but Anwar is part of the process that makes recommendations. If he supports the Pardons Board's decision to recommend a pardon for Najib, he might

---

save the coalition alliance, but would be criticised for doing so and his reputation would suffer. Other members of the alliance may withdraw their support. On the other hand, if the recommendation is to refuse a pardon, UMNO would not forgive him for failing to help Najib. In either case, he loses.

There are also the criminal charges against former prime minister Muhyiddin Yassin, Anwar's chief rival for the premiership after the last election, which some critics suggest have as much to do with politics as tackling corruption. Anwar has repeatedly denied directing or interfering in the Malaysian Anti-Corruption Commission's (MACC's) investigations.[6]

Allegations of corruption and cronyism are not unusual in Malaysia. It applies to every political party. Several members of Anwar's own PH coalition, including former sports minister Syed Saddiq Syed Abdul Rahman and DAP national chairman Lim Guan Eng, are also on trial for corruption-related charges.

It should not be forgotten that Anwar's predecessors as prime minister, Muhyiddin Yassin and Ismail Sabri Yaakob, tried not to interfere in the court cases of both Najib and Zahid. When they refused to help, both were toppled by UMNO, through the withdrawal of support for Muhyiddin and the dissolution of parliament for Ismail.

If UMNO is to retaliate by withdrawing its support for Anwar, then the result would be that Anwar would have to resign as prime minister or dissolve parliament. The likely candidate for the new prime minister would be deputy prime minister Zahid, but that would depend on whether he could stitch a coalition together, which seems unlikely. The odds are Anwar would prefer to go to the polls and take his chances at another election.

In his interview with me on 27 January 2023, Anwar stated that his support had increased, saying the "late entry was Sarawak, and Sarawak is

---

6   Al Jazeera, 10 March 2023

now solid, more solid than even UMNO, with us. Now us, and Sarawak alone, are already the simple majority. And with BN is quite strong." The reality of that is yet to be seen.

MAHATHIR-ANWAR FEUD INTENSIFIES

Mahathir is no longer a political threat in the sense of wielding power by leading a political party or by holding a parliamentary seat. However, he is not without influence. Many still support and respect him for his economic achievements, mostly the Malay community. At almost 98 years of age, one would have thought he would just quietly fade away, but he is as vociferous as ever.

When Mahathir hates, he hates utterly. We saw that in his campaigns against his successors as prime minister, Abdullah Badawi and Najib Razak, with whom he could never be satisfied. He joined the PH alliance in 2018 to remove Najib from power, on the basis that if the alliance won the government, he would become prime minister. But it became obvious over time that he was never going to step aside as prime minister to allow Anwar to succeed him in 2020, which is why he engineered the leadership crisis by resigning, with the expectation that he would be reappointed.

That crafty manoeuvre failed when Muhyiddin and Azmin Ali realised they did not need Mahathir to seize power and formed their own alliance with UMNO. The government only failed when UMNO withdrew its support.

Mahathir constantly criticises Anwar and the government from the sidelines, stirring up trouble with the Malays, where his support is greatest and where Anwar's support is weakest. The feud between them intensified when Anwar, while making a speech to the PKR Congress on 18 March 2023, referred to someone "who in the past had been in power for 22 years and an additional 22 months" taking advantage of his position to make his family and himself wealthier.

Anwar did not mention any names, but said that the same person was also attempting to stoke hatred among the Malay Muslim majority towards other races by claiming they had lost power under the current government. Mahathir had been actively involved in stirring up opposition within the Malay community to the PH government.

Mahathir responded saying it was obvious that Anwar was referring to him and that he wanted an apology, otherwise he would sue him for his slanderous remarks. On his Facebook page, he said he had put up with years of slander from Anwar "but now that he is the prime minister, he maintains his accusations. So, I have asked him to retract (his statements), failing which I shall take legal action."

Anwar refused to apologise, saying he would produce evidence in court to support his corruption claims. He is reported as saying: "I don't want to fight. He has asked for proof, I will give (him) proof, no problem."[7]

Mahathir responded by filing a defamation claim seeking US$32.3 million in damages. The former prime minister said that "the statements were made by Anwar in his capacity as prime minister, which had a more devastating effect than any other individual in Malaysia." Anwar responded, saying he was "leaving it to his lawyers to handle it."[8]

However, he later filed a defence to the defamation claim, saying: "[Mahathir's] malicious and baseless attacks on the present government led by the defendant (Anwar) is an attempt to redeem himself politically at any cost." That includes "instigating racial turbulence and undermining political, economic and social stability, (which) has led to him to no longer be perceived as a credible person."[9]

The defence filed by Anwar's lawyers further stated that: "Mahathir's administration was marred by numerous corruption and financial scandals, repeated efforts to curb the freedom of speech, political dissent and attacks on the Malaysian judiciary as well as the rule of law."

---

7   Malaysiakini, 7 April 2023
8   *The Star*, 6 May 2023
9   FMT, 15 June 2023

Anwar said Dr Mahathir had made decisions which encouraged the practice of cronyism in the country, especially during his first tenure as Prime Minister and Minister of Finance. He said there were "reasonable grounds to believe that Dr Mahathir had used his position to procure financial benefit and enrich his family members and cronies." He said Dr Mahathir "had used the Bumiputera agenda to enrich his own family members and cronies, which led to a negative impact and downturn on the nation's economy and finances."[10]

He went on to cite several decisions made by Dr Mahathir Mohamad to justify why the RM150 million defamation suit against him by the latter should be thrown out, listing "examples of decisions made by Dr Mahathir during his 22-year tenure as prime minister for the first time from 1981 to 2003, and again from 2018 to 2020 which protected business personalities closely linked to him."

These examples included:

1. Mahathir's direction to Anwar (who was then Minister of Finance) in 1997 to devise a special scheme to bail out a company (KPB) owned by his son Mirzan, which Anwar refused to do. Anwar was later informed that Mahathir had directed Petronas to proceed with the bailout plan.
2. Awarding a Telekom Malaysia Bhd contract worth RM214 million to Opcom Cables Sdn Bhd, a company with Mahathir's sons and daughter-in-law as directors. The contract was awarded four days after Mahathir became prime minister in 2018, and before the formation of a new Cabinet and without its approval.
3. Mahathir's attempted bailout of the Perwaja Group, which suffered massive losses in 1995, leaving the Ministry of Finance with financial exposure of more than RM6 billion.

10 *New Straits Times*, 15 June 2023, 2.57pm

Finally, Anwar pleaded that Mahathir had every opportunity during his tenure as prime minister, "to create and implement policies to uplift the Malays". "Instead, when no longer in power now, he raises these issues in an attempt to undermine the defendant [Anwar] and to remain politically relevant," he said.[11]

He went on to say, "Instead of prioritising the welfare of the Malays, the plaintiff's tenure as Prime Minister was tainted with various financial controversies including bailouts and privatisation policies which benefited a selected few, as opposed to the Malay community at large."

Anwar is relying on the defence of justification, fair comment, qualified privilege and free speech as guaranteed under Article 10 of the Federal Constitution.

Therefore, the impending court case promises to be a dramatic showdown between the former foes and is just one of the challenges faced by the prime minister as he settles into office.

At the same time, Anwar had in late 2022 brought defamation proceedings against Muhyiddin Yassin, claiming that the former prime minister had slandered him while campaigning for the Padang Serai parliamentary seat at the 2022 general election. Muhyiddin claimed that Anwar had received RM15 million from the Selangor state government when serving as its economic advisor. That action is heading for trial with the parties lodging their pleadings (court documents) in early 2023.

There is a long "tradition" in Malaysia of politicians suing each other for alleged defamatory remarks. The Malaysian Federal Court in March 2021 ruled that a person cannot be sued for a defamatory comment made against a political party, although it was not a blanket immunity from other laws of the country that target public speeches and messages. However, this ruling does not prevent cases being brought against individual persons. A legal fight has the potential to distract Malaysians from more important issues.

---

11 *New Straits Times*, 15 June 2023, 3.59pm

THE FIRST SIX MONTHS OF GOVERNMENT

Much was expected of the "unity government" cobbled together by Anwar after GE15 in November 2022. There were the usual tensions inherent with the reality that no single party had achieved a parliamentary majority. The national election had increased the divisive racial divide between the Malays and others, which was a wedge that had been successfully exploited by PAS and PN.

Malaysia's most pressing problem was the economy, which had suffered from excessive corruption and cronyism under the Najib government, but it had not really been effectively tackled either by the Pakatan Harapan government after its election in 2018, or the Perikatan Nasional regime that followed it.

Importantly, there was the increasingly high cost of living that impacted upon the nation's low-income earners, who for decades had been propped up by subsidies for such things as fuel, electricity and food. These subsidies were provided to all citizens. In 2022, the cost of government subsidies was RM80 billion.

Prime Minister Najib during his administration had brought down the level of subsidies for certain items, but it wasn't only an economic problem – funding the so-called "rural poor" was a political tool as well, intended to maintain Malay support for the ruling party.

When Anwar came to power in November 2022, he announced a review of the extensive system of subsidies, aiming to focus more effectively on lower-income groups. He said that "subsidies must be targeted, otherwise those subsidies are enjoyed not just by the low-income group, but also the wealthy."[12]

One difficulty in tackling the huge cost of subsidies is the reluctance of the population to pay more for basic essentials, if subsidies are removed or reduced. It will take some effort to wean Malaysians off this system of subsidies that has been entrenched for decades.

---

12   Reuters, 27 November 2022

The further problem for Anwar is that he needs to cultivate and draw more political support from the Malays, who benefit most from this system. He needs to limit the government's intervention in the economy, particularly its interference on prices. He needs more than rhetoric to do that.

For years, Malaysia has suffered from the "brain-drain" of young Malaysians who have taken their skills away by migrating overseas for better job opportunities. It's all about financial stability, and how Malaysians see a future for themselves in their own country.

There is no doubting Anwar's clear agenda to attract foreign investment, which is essential for developing a healthy and thriving economy. Elsewhere, I have detailed his trips to Malaysia's neighbours, and in particular China. These trips have been highly successful in not only attracting investment, but in building better bilateral relationships, which had lacked priority in previous governments.

There were also visits by foreign nations to Malaysia. On 21 May 2023, the Crown Prince of Abu Dhabi began a four-day special visit. He met with the King and Prime Minister Anwar. The United Arab Emirates (UAE) is Malaysia's second largest trading partner and export destination, as well as the second largest import destination in the West Asia region. In 2022, Malaysia's total trade with the UAE rose by 73 per cent to RM38.73 billion from RM22.33 billion the year before.[13]

The main challenge for Malaysia is good governance and fighting corruption, after years of cronyism and mismanagement of the country. Anwar has been particularly vocal about these issues. In our interview of 27 January 2023, he spoke of the magnitude of the corruption, that even surprised him. He is progressive and reform-minded, but viewed with suspicion by more conservative elements that are worried about his liberal tendencies and agenda for reform.

---

13 *The Star*, 21 May 2023

There is also an entrenched system of corruption and cronyism whereby the only way to do business is by underhand bribes and payments, which has extended to the most senior political leaders and businessmen. It's a cultural issue in Malaysia. Paying bribes is accepted as the price of doing business, and it saps the economic life blood of the country.

There are just too many vested interests in Malaysia that are opposed to change, and that is a major hurdle for Anwar to overcome. Recall that in our interview of 27 January 2023, he spoke of the threats that had been made against him since becoming prime minister after he had voiced the need to fight corruption and cronyism.

As one taxi driver complained to me: "We don't mind them taking ten per cent of money (from corruption), but not 60 per cent." In that statement was, sadly, an acceptance that this was the way in Malaysia, but also an expression that it has gone too far. Maybe the people are ready for change, but self-interest is a powerful motivator in opposing change.

Undoubtedly, Anwar needs to give Malaysia more confidence in itself and develop and promote a concrete vision for the country, which has grown tired of political machinations and tribal politics. That surely must come about through a period of political stability, sensible reform and good governance.

Anwar is aware that there is a high expectation that he will be different from others who have led Malaysia. It is only a few months since he became prime minister, which is too soon to judge his government. If he is able to secure confidence in his government by attracting international investment to revive the economy, eradicating extreme poverty and reducing the cost of living, then that will happen and there is every chance he will last his full term of five years.

There are six state assembly elections that must be held by June to July 2023. It will be regarded as a test of the popularity of the country's ruling coalition. Anwar's greatest challenge is increasing his coalition's vote share with the Malays. Pundits say it is not possible that he could secure any of the northern states, and that he will need to consolidate his own strongholds, especially Selangor.

These contests must be viewed against a backdrop where the opposition parties are playing race politics and pushing populist causes. Losing Selangor or Negeri Sembilan would be a significant blow for Anwar, but even if he suffers losses, he should not be written off as his unity government seems secure for the time being, having bolstered his support from Sarawak and Sabah.

CAN THE PAKATAN HARAPAN ALLIANCE SURVIVE?

On 19 December 2022, Anwar won the vote of confidence in parliament, which stabilised the alliance, and the community's perception that in the early life of the government, all was going well. It was vital backing for his premiership, but as Anwar himself said in our interview of 27 January 2023, that "it's early days", so he understands he must deliver on his promises, and his need to focus on key issues.

Anwar also needs to cultivate and increase the support of the Malays for his administration, which was about 17 per cent support at the last general election. Some have suggested that UMNO is best placed to do that, despite its dismal failure to hold on to many of its parliamentary seats.

As referred to at the start of this chapter, Anwar had conceded in our interview of 2018 that "it will be a major challenge" to work with a coalition, as evidenced by their historical track record and acknowledged the need to exert greater effort to overcome the inherent issues.

Unlike Mahathir, however, Anwar has consistently demonstrated his capacity to negotiate and reach compromises that will hold the competing views and ambitions of diverse groups of separate parties together. This ability will be essential not only for controlling the component members of his government, but also for focusing their ambitions towards advancing a coherent and reformist agenda. So far, so good, but Malaysian politics has in recent years been an unpredictable roller-coaster ride.

CHAPTER 12

The Film "Anwar: The Untold Story"

Not many people have a movie made about them while they are still alive. Anwar Ibrahim is one such person. It must be said that his life has been a roller-coaster ride of dramatic highs and lows over the last 20 years or so. Such is the nature of politics in Malaysia.

My previous books documented Anwar's dramatic sacking as deputy prime minister by Mahathir in 1998, leading to a conviction for sodomy, which was successfully overturned on appeal in 2004. Then came his release after six years in prison and with it the prospect of a political comeback, but just as that happened, he was charged again with sodomy, acquitted after trial, and then convicted after two appeals.

After another four years in prison, he was finally released, having been granted an unconditional royal pardon in 2018. What followed were two tumultuous years in government and opposition, and then after a federal election in November 2022, he managed to cobble together a "unity government", resulting in his appointment as prime minister.

Plenty of material there for a film. Political cartoonist Zulkiflee Anwar Haque, also known by his pen name of "Zunar", did just that. He put together a joint-venture film project with Indonesian filmmakers and actors depicting the life of Anwar from the time of his appointment as deputy prime minister until his sacking and assault by the Inspector-General of Police, after having been arrested and taken into custody.

The film ends with the iconic image of a black-eyed Anwar being led by police through a large crowd of supporters with his arm raised in a gesture of defiance. The main point of the film is his stand against corruption and the strength of his relationship with his wife, Wan Azizah, and the difficulties faced by his family during that time. It was the start of the *Reformasi* movement.

"Anwar: The Untold Story" was directed by Viva Westi and stars Farid Kamil Zahari as Anwar, and Indonesian actress Acha Septriasa as Wan Azizah, with Hasnul Rahmat playing Mahathir. The film opened on over 1,000 screens in 120 cinemas across Malaysia, reportedly taking in RM1 million on opening day.

The film premiered on the evening of 8 May 2023, at the DADI cinema at the Pavilion Complex at Bukit Bintang, with more than 250 guests. Anwar paid tribute to his wife, later saying: "The love and strength of a wife and mother fuel[led] the torch of struggle." In a touching moment, when the lights went up after the film ended, Anwar embraced his wife and tenderly kissed her.

Prime Minister Anwar Ibrahim embraces Wan Azizah at the film premiere. Photo from Anwar's Facebook page.

In the press conference that followed immediately after the screening, Anwar said that watching the film with his wife and family reminded him of what they went through during the dark days of his imprisonment. He said he took the advice of his wife to control his emotions, and that the only time he shed a tear during his incarceration was on the death of his mother. "I just couldn't control it; at other times, I had to smile through my tears," he said.[1]

However, he told the media and the crowd that stayed after the screening of the film to hear him speak that, "It is difficult for me to comment much as I have tried very hard to forget certain episodes which were too hurtful for me to bear." He went on to say he would not let the hardship stop him from campaigning for what was right. "The battle against corruption continues. As prime minister, I want to save this country, fight against corruption, and fight it hard," he stated.[2]

1   *The Star*, 10 May 2023
2   KiniTV, 9 May 2023

Cartoon by Zunar

Acknowledgements

There have been three books before the publication of *Anwar Triumphs*. In the last book, I expressed my thanks for the contribution and support many organisations provided in sponsoring my role as an observer at the trial and appeals of Anwar Ibrahim over the last 22 years. These include the Geneva-based Inter-Parliamentary Union, LAWASIA, the International Commission of Jurists (ICJ), the Law Council of Australia, the Australian Bar Association (ABA), the Union Internationale des Avocats (UIA) and the Commonwealth Lawyers Association.

This publication really brings together these roller-coaster events into what many might think is a conclusion of a long and continuing struggle for justice. But given the nature of politics in Malaysia, it may only be the "end of the beginning", as Winston Churchill once said, with more to come.

May I thank those who have made this book possible, including the wonderful Datuk David Yeoh, whose advice and support has been invaluable. I must also thank publisher Marshall Cavendish International, which has published all of my books. Special mention of Melvin Neo, Mindy Pang, Anita Russell and Lee Mei Lin, all of whom contributed to making my disjointed writings into a readable narrative. Finally, thanks to Pansing Books, which once again has agreed to sell, market and distribute this book.

About the Author

Mark Trowell is a leading Australian criminal lawyer. He was appointed Queen's Counsel in 2000. He has been a defence lawyer for most of his career, but has also prosecuted criminal cases for the Director of Public Prosecutions. He has appeared as counsel at two Royal Commissions. In December 2006, he was appointed by the Australian Government to undertake a review of the legislation governing the Australian Crime Commission.

He is co-chair of the criminal law standing committee of LAWASIA. Over the last 20 years, he has been an international observer reporting for several law organisations at the criminal proceedings against veteran Malaysian advocate the late Karpal Singh, Minister Rishad Bathiudeen of Sri Lanka and UDD Leader Jatuporn Prompan in Thailand. He has also represented the interests of the Geneva-based Inter-Parliamentary Union at the criminal trials and appeals of opposition leaders Anwar Ibrahim in Malaysia and General Sarath Fonseka in Sri Lanka.

Mark is the author of three bestselling books, *Sodomy II: The Trials of Anwar Ibrahim* (2012), *The Prosecution of Anwar Ibrahim: The Final Play* (2015) and *Anwar Returns: The Final Twist* (2018).